The Beaver Book of War Stories

Warfare in all its aspects – from fighting on land, sea and in the air, to the lonely and heroic work of Resistance agents and a daring escape from a prison camp – is the subject of these stories. They appear in chronological order, from Gallipoli in May 1915 to the Red Devils at Arnhem in September 1944, and all are tales of human courage in the midst of desperate and often tragic circumstances.

George Kay has written a large number of books for both children and adults, including *The Beaver Book of Games* and *Collecting Pebbles, Rocks and Fossils*. He lives in Buckinghamshire.

The background photograph on the cover shows sappers opening the way through the minefields at the Battle of El Alamein on the night of 23 October 1942, and is from the painting by Terence Cuneo

The black and white photographs show (*from left to right, and from the back cover to the front*):

1 Battle of Britain: RAF fighter squadron at the double
2 Western Desert: South African troops advancing towards the enemy through a smokescreen
3 Western Desert: a German tank advancing during the fighting
4 A German mobilised column crossing the desert
5 The *Admiral Graf Spee* in flames off Montevideo
6 A formation of Spitfires

THE BEAVER BOOK OF
WAR
STORIES

George Kay

Illustrated by Peter Dennis

Beaver Books

First published in 1981 by
The Hamlyn Publishing Group Limited
London · New York · Sydney · Toronto
Astronaut House, Feltham, Middlesex, England
(Paperback Division: Hamlyn Paperbacks, Banda House,
Cambridge Grove, Hammersmith, London W6 0LE)

© Copyright this collection George Kay 1981
© Copyright Illustrations The Hamlyn Publishing Group
Limited 1981
ISBN 0 600 20362 X

Reproduced, printed and bound in Great Britain by
Hazell Watson & Viney Ltd, Aylesbury, Bucks

*The original Imperial measurements have been
retained in the extracts in this book
as they are often technical terms which cannot
be converted precisely to metric.*

Contents

Acknowledgements

The author and publishers would like to thank the following people for giving permission to include in this anthology material which is their copyright:

William Collins Sons & Company Limited for 'The Battle of the River Plate' from *The Battle of the Atlantic* by John Costello and Terry Hughes

Bryan Cooper and Bolt & Watson Limited for 'The First Tank Battle' from *Tank Battles of World War I* by Bryan Cooper, published by Ian Allan Limited

William Heinemann Limited for the extract from *Cockleshell Heroes* by C. E. Lucas Phillips; and for 'The Night of 23 October 1942' from *Alamein* by C. E. Lucas Phillips

David Higham Associates Limited for 'The Arrest of the White Rabbit' from *The White Rabbit* by Bruce Marshall, published by Evans Brothers Limited

Michael Joseph Limited and Curtis Brown Limited for 'The Red Devils at Arnhem' from *The Red Beret* by Hilary St George Saunders

John Murray (Publishers) Limited for 'The Chindits at Blackpool, Burma' from *Chindit* by Richard Rhodes James

Laurence Pollinger Limited for 'The Nine Hours' Truce at Anzac Cove' from *Gallipoli* by Alan Moorehead, published by Hamish Hamilton Limited

Mrs Nancy Rivett for 'Battle of the Java Sea' from *Behind Bamboo* by Rohan Deakin Rivett, published by Angus & Robertson Limited

Edward H. Sims for 'One of the Few' from his book *The Fighter Pilots*, published by Cassell Limited

Jerrard Tickell Publications Limited for 'Odette, GC' from *Odette* by Jerrard Tickell, published by Kaye & Ward Limited

Eric Williams for the extract from his book *The Wooden Horse*, published by William Collins Sons & Company Limited

The diagram on page 131 is Crown copyright and is reproduced by kind permission of the Controller of Her Majesty's Stationery Office

INTRODUCTION

No sensible person loves war. It is evil. Like all evils, if and when it comes, men and women throughout mankind's history have fought to end it, for almost as great as our love of life is our love of liberty. That the warriors on both sides of a conflict believe they are in the right does not detract from their courage. We can honour brave people whatever the rights and wrongs of the cause they believed it was their duty to defend and even die for.

The most imaginative writers of fiction cannot possibly devise plots as enthralling as those of true stories of warfare; nor can they portray the characters of such extraordinary people as the heroes – and villains – who go to battle.

In these stories you will not read of easy victories by those we may regard as the goodies over the baddies. Often the chances of winning were remote and glorious failure almost inevitable. And the men and women whose adventurous exploits you can share as you read this book were ordinary people caught up in the turmoil of war. They did their duty as they knew it to be, not intimidated by the danger which would accompany their actions, so that we might live in peace. Their stories enable us to ask ourselves: would we be as courageous as they were if we found ourselves in the same situation?

Selection of the stories occupied many months of enthralling reading, marred only by regret that so many accounts of high adventure and outstanding valour had to be omitted. Those that have been chosen will be a spur to you to read the complete books from which they have been taken, and to explore for yourself the almost inexhaustible treasure-trove of true tales of warfare – from the Wooden Horse of Troy in 1184 BC to the Wooden Horse of a German prison camp in 1944; from the defeat of the invading Spanish Armada in 1588 to the Air Battle which saved Britain in 1940. Each story has its special appeal, its unique plot, but all have the same theme: the tragedy and drama when war comes.

THE NINE HOURS' TRUCE AT
ANZAC COVE

Cape Suvla
salt lake
Suvla Bay
Anzac Cove
GALLIPOLI PENINSULA
Cape Tekke
BLACK SEA
BULGARIA
Istanbul
Dardanelles
Cape Helles
GREECE
TURKEY

◤ Landing beaches
∿ Turkish defences

MEDITERRANEAN SEA

On 25 April, 1915, an Allied invasion fleet of 200
warships, troop transports and supply vessels brought
30 000 Australians and New Zealanders, 17 000 British,
16 000 French, and 10 000 Royal Navy personnel, with
1 600 pack animals, 300 vehicles, and a vast supply of
armaments, to the beaches of Gallipoli. The invasion
zone was a wild and rock-strewn peninsula forming the
southern shore on the European side of the Dardanelles,
the waterway linking the Mediterranean and the Black
Sea. The object of the greatest sea-borne assault of the
war was to strike at the heart of the Turkish Ottoman
Empire and to open a supply route to the hard-pressed
Russians in the war on Germany's eastern front.

General Sir Ian Hamilton was Commander-in-Chief

of the expedition, with the British General Sir William Birdwood in command of the Australian and New Zealand Army Corps which landed on the narrow beach, later immortalised as a symbol of tenacious courage as Anzac Cove.

On the Turkish side the German Field Marshal Otto Liman von Sanders was Commander-in-Chief of the Turkish forces. His most brilliant officer was Mustafa Kemal, the future leader of Turkey. Essad Pasha commanded the Turkish corps defending the area behind Anzac Cove.

Poor intelligence about the strength of the Turkish defences and the almost insuperable slopes and deep gullies above the beach-heads, plus confusion in the high command, contributed to the tragedy of Gallipoli. By the time this story comes to the night of 18 May the number of Anzac troops had been reduced to 12 500 fit for battle. Against them the enemy had massed a force of 42 000, with orders to annihilate the invaders by nightfall.

The Anzac position had by now become very clearly defined: it was a shallow triangle, covering about 400 acres, its base, a mile and a half long, resting on the sea, its apex reaching to the slopes of Sari Bair about a thousand yards from the shore. In order to avoid the fire of the British Fleet the Turks had dug their trenches almost on top of the Anzac lines, and at some places the two sides were divided by not more than ten yards. The situation at Quinn's and Courtnay's Posts in the centre of the line was fantastic; directly behind the Australian trench (which was kept packed with men by day and night), a steep cliff fell away to the gully below, and the Turks had only to make an advance of five yards in order to drive a wedge through the bridgehead to the sea. But this they never could succeed in doing though they attacked repeatedly during the first half of May. No-man's-land at these and other points was no larger than a small room, and it was the easiest thing in the world for the Turks to toss a hand grenade into the Anzac trenches. The only real defence against this was to throw the grenade smartly back again before it exploded: except for a few jam tins which were filled with explosive at a makeshift workshop on the beach, the Australians had no such weapons of their own. No man could expose the smallest fraction of his body for an instant without being shot, and even a periscope hoisted for a moment above the parapet was immediately shattered. An extreme tension prevailed in the bridgehead; there was no hour when some new raid was not expected or delivered, no minute when shells were not crashing among them or bullets screaming overhead. The soldiers managed to sleep through this racket at odd hours of the day and night, but it was never a sufficient rest. No one was ever safe. On 14 May General Bridges, the commander of the Australian Division, was mortally wounded, and the following day Birdwood had his hair parted by a bullet while he was looking through a periscope. The wound turned septic and was very painful but he continued in command.

There was an intense hatred of the Turks among the Dominion soldiers. Most of them had grown up in a world of clear and obvious values; a fight was a fight, you knew who your enemy was and you stood up to him and had it out, fairly and squarely, in the open. It was in this spirit that they had volunteered for service in the Army. The charge was the thing, the quick and palpable blow in the face that knocked the man down. War, in fact, was an extension of the pub brawl, and it had in it the elements of rioting, of street fighting, of instant physical revenge.

But nothing of the kind had happened at Gallipoli. From the day they had landed the soldiers had scarcely ever seen the enemy; he lurked unseen in the heights above, he sniped down on them and caught them unawares, he stood back at a safe distance with his guns and burst his shrapnel above their heads, and there seemed to be no effective way of retaliating. After more than three weeks of this the soldiers were beginning to feel an increasing sense of frustration and of impotent anger in their narrow bridgehead. A claustrophobia had developed; they felt that they had been caught in a trap, and there seemed to be something unfair in this kind of fighting in which they were never given a chance of showing their real courage and their strength.

Beyond this there was at this early stage another and perhaps deeper feeling that there was a monstrosity and inhumanity about the Turks; they were cruel and sinister fanatics, capable of any sort of vice and bestiality – in brief, it was the popular picture that had been drawn of them by Byron and the emotions of Gladstonian liberal England. The Turks were 'natives' – but natives of a peculiarly dangerous and subtle kind. And so the Australian and New Zealand soldiers fought, not an ordinary man, but a monster prefigured by imagination and by propaganda; and they hated him.

Despite these things, perhaps even because of them, an extraordinary cheerfulness and exaltation possessed the men in the front line. Living with the instant prospect of death, all pettiness, all the normal anxieties and jealousies of life, deserted them, and they developed an almost mystical feeling towards the extreme danger that surrounded them. The fighting became an elaborate and exciting game in which they were all immensely engrossed, and it was only when they were retired to rest for a while in some half-haven under the cliffs that they became aware again of the miseries of their situation, the monotonous food, the endless physical discomfort, the impossible limits of a life in which even a canteen of fresh water or a bathe in the sea were the utmost luxuries.

By now death had become a familiar, and they often talked about it in a half-derisive deprecating slang. In the same way as the Chinese will laugh at other people's pain it became a huge joke when the men bathing off the beach were caught in a burst of shrapnel, or when some poor devil had his head blown off while he was in the latrine. There had to be some sort of expression which would help to rationalise the unbearable circumstances of their lives, some way of obtaining relief from the shock of it all, and since tears were impossible this callous hard-boiled laughter became the thing. They were not fatalists. They believed that a mistake had been made in the landing at Gaba Tepe and that they might easily have to pay for it with their lives; but they very much wanted to go on living, they were all for the battle and they hoped and believed obscurely that in the end they would win.

These high spirits, this fineness and integrity created by the powerful drug of risk, might not perhaps have continued indefinitely under such a strain, but there had certainly been no weakening in morale when, on 18 May, the soldiers became aware that something unusual was happening in the enemy lines. An unaccountable silence spread through the hills before them. For the first time since they had landed the fearful racket of the Turkish howitzers died away, and for several minutes at a stretch no rifle or machine-gun was fired. In this strange quiet most of the day went by. Then at five o'clock in the evening a tremendous artillery barrage broke out, and it continued for about half an hour. It chanced that on this day a naval aircraft had been sent out to fix the position of an enemy warship in the straits, and on his return the pilot reported that he had seen large numbers of men massing behind the Turkish lines. Later in the day this information was confirmed by a second pilot who had also seen enemy soldiers coming across the straits in boats from the Asiatic side; and from the battleship *Triumph* there was a further report that Turkish reinforcements were marching north from Cape Helles to the Anzac front. On hearing this, Birdwood sent a message to his two divisional commanders warning them to expect an attack that night; the men were to stand to arms at 3 a.m., which was half an hour before the usual time.

The night turned cold and misty, and when the moon went down at 11.35 p.m. there was hardly a sound along the front except for the breaking of the waves on the shore. Suddenly at fifteen minutes to midnight, a fusillade of rifle fire which was heavier than anything that had been heard before burst out from the Turkish trenches, and as it spread along the line the Anzac commanders kept telephoning to their outposts to ask if they were being attacked. But nothing followed, and presently the uproar dwindled into silence again. At 3 a.m. the men were roused, and they took their places on the firing steps with their bayonets fixed to their rifles. It was still cold and most of them were wearing their overcoats.

Hardly five minutes had gone by when a shout of warning went up from one of the outposts, and a company of Turks was seen advancing down a ravine known as Wire Gully in the centre of the line. There had been no preliminary bugle call, none of the usual shouts of Allah, Allah: merely these shadowy forms in the half-darkness and the long line of bayonets. The Australians opened fire from either side of the gully, and immediately the enemy bugles sounded and the charge began. Everywhere along the line the Turks jumped up from their hiding places and in a dark cloud swept forward over the broken ground.

At most places the oncoming enemy had to cross two or three hundred yards before they reached the Anzac entrenchments, and so there was a half a minute or more when they were exposed in the open and quite defenceless. Very few of them survived even that amount of time. There was a kind of cascading movement in the battle; directly one line of soldiers had come over the parapet and been destroyed another line formed up, emerged into view and was cut down. For the first hour it was simply a matter of indiscriminate killing, but presently the Australians and New Zealanders began to adopt more systematic methods: when a Turkish officer appeared they deliberately withheld their fire until he had assembled the full company of his men in the open. Then all were destroyed together. At some points it became a kind of game to pick off the survivors as they ran back and forth across the battlefield like terrified rabbits in search of cover. Here and there some few of the Turks did manage to get into the Anzac trenches, but they survived only for a few minutes; there was a quick and awful bayoneting and then the tide receded again.

As daylight broke the battle assumed the character of a hunt, with the Turkish officers serving in the role of beaters driving the game on to the guns. A wild, almost berserk excitement filled the Australian and New Zealand ranks. In order to get a better view many of the soldiers jumped up and sat astride the parapets and from there they blazed away at the screaming mass of Turks before them. The Anzac soldiers who had been held in reserve could not bear to be left out of the fight; they came pressing forward offering to pay for a place on the firing line. In one trench two soldiers actually fought one another with their fists for a vacant position on the parapet, and there was a kind of mad surrealism in the shouts and cries along the line as each new Turkish rush came on. 'Backsheesh' 'Imshi Yallah', 'Eggs is cooked'.[1] Once an Australian was heard shouting to the Turks as they fell back from his trench, '*Saida* (goodbye). Play you again next Saturday.'

By 5 a.m., when a hot sun was beginning to stream down on to the battlefield, the attack was broken. But the orders to the Turks were that they should continue the fight until they got through to the sea, and so they went on with the struggle for another six hours, each new charge getting a little feebler than the last. Mustafa Kemal had been reduced to the command of a single division, the 19th, for the period of the offensive, and he alone, of the four divisional commanders engaged, had succeeded in making any headway. When at midday Essad Pasha decided to break off the action 10 000 of his men had fallen, and of these some 5 000, dead, dying and wounded, were lying out in the open between the trenches.

Other heavier battles than this were fought at Gallipoli, but none with such a terrible concentration of killing, none so one-sided, and none with so strange an aftermath. Through the long afternoon the wounded lay with the dead on the battlefield, and although the trenches on either side were only a yard or two away no one could go out and bring them in without taking the risk of being instantly shot.

'No sound came from that dreadful space,' the Australian history of the campaign relates, 'but here and there some wounded or dying man, silently lying without help or any hope of it under the sun which glared from a cloudless sky, turned painfully from one side to the other, or slowly raised an arm towards heaven.'

Birdwood was warned by his medical staff that, quite apart from any feelings of humanity, the dead should be buried as quickly as possible to prevent infection spreading through the Army. When the afternoon had passed without any sign of the Turks renewing the attack, he sent off Aubrey Herbert to ask Hamilton aboard the *Arcadian* if he might arrange an armistice.

Herbert was an odd figure on the Anzac bridgehead – indeed, he would have been odd in any army on any battlefield: a Member of Parliament turned soldier, an eccentric, a poet and a scholar, who, far from hating the Turks, was captivated by them. This did not mean he was disloyal – he was determined that they should be defeated – but he knew Turkey and Turkish very well, and he believed that with better handling by the politicians they might have been converted into allies. Of all the band who had been with Rupert Brooke at Alexandria he was the one most possessed of ideas, and despite his short-sightedness, his impulsive and agitated manner, he was very brave and saw very clearly under the façade of things. Hamilton was glad enough to have him on his staff as an intelligence officer with the rank of lieutenant-colonel, but he noted in his diary that he was 'excessively unorthodox'.

Herbert chose to do his intelligence work in the front line at Anzac, and he proceeded to war in the manner of a nineteenth-century gentleman-adventurer. Servants were engaged at Lemnos,[2] suitable horses and mules acquired, an adequate kit assembled, and off he went with an extraordinary assemblage of Greek and Levantine interpreters to the peninsula. There were staff troubles almost at once. A spy mania was raging through the Anzac bridgehead – the fear of spies seems to be endemic in every crisis in every military campaign – and his interpreters were arrested as many as four and five times a day. A terrible hail of shrapnel once fell on Herbert's dugout, and the cook, a Greek named Christopher of the Black Lamp, with the tears pouring down his face gave two hours' notice, though why it should be two hours and not two minutes he was unable to explain. Among these and other domestic anxieties Herbert continued with his work of questioning the Turkish prisoners and of acting as a kind of general confidant of the commanders in all questions relating to the habits and character of the enemy.

His methods of propaganda were very direct. He crawled into the foremost trenches and from there he addressed the enemy soldiers in their own language, urging them to desert, promising them good treatment and pointing out that the real quarrel of the Allies was not with Turkey but with the Germans. At times he actually got into trenches which communicated directly into the enemy emplacements, and lying on the dead bodies there, he called to the Turks through a single barrier of sandbags. Occasionally they would listen and enter into argument with him. More often they replied with hand-grenades – a thing which did not make Herbert very welcome with the Anzac troops – and in Constantinople one of the newspapers announced that there was someone in the Anzac bridgehead who was making a low attempt to lure the Turks from their duty by imitating the prayers of the muezzin.

It now fell to Herbert to put the case to Hamilton for an armistice. He argued that unless something was done quickly the situation would become intolerable: our own wounded as well as Turkish were still lying in the open, and in the hot sun the dead bodies were decomposing rapidly. Hamilton answered that he would not initiate any proposal himself, because the enemy would make propaganda of it, but if the Turks liked to come forward he was willing to grant them a cessation of hostilities for a limited period. It was agreed finally that notes could be thrown into the Turkish trenches telling them of this.

Meanwhile all 20 May had gone by and unknown to Hamilton and Herbert the soldiers at the front had already taken matters into their own hands. Towards evening an Australian colonel caused a Red Cross flag to be hoisted on a plateau at the lower end of the line. He intended to send out his stretcher-bearers to bring in a number of wounded Turks who were crying out pitiably in front of his trenches. Before they could move, however, the Turks put two bullets through the staff of the flag and brought it down. A moment later a man jumped up from the Turkish trenches and came running across no-man's-land. He stopped on the parapet above the Australians' heads, spoke a few words of apology, and then ran back to his own lines again. Immediately afterwards Red Crescent flags appeared above the enemy trenches, and Turkish stretcher-bearers came out. All firing ceased along the line, and in this eerie stillness General Walker, the commander of the 1st Australian Division, got up and walked towards the enemy. A group of Turkish officers came out to meet him, and for a while they stood there in the open, smoking, and talking in French. It was agreed that they should exchange letters on the subject of an armistice at 8 p.m. that night.

While this was going on another impromptu parley with the enemy had opened on another section of the line. It was now growing late and Birdwood, as soon as he heard what was happening, issued an order that no further burials were to be made that night. A note signed by the General's A.D.C. was handed to a Turkish officer: 'If you want a truce to bury your dead,' it said, 'send a staff officer, under a flag of truce, to our headquarters via the Gaba Tepe road, between 10 a.m. and 12 noon tomorrow.'

At this stage neither side seems to have been absolutely sure of themselves; there was a tense feeling that some act of treachery might occur at any moment, that an attack might be launched under the cover of the white flags – and indeed, an Australian soldier who had been out in no-man's-land came back with the report that the enemy trenches were filled with men who were apparently ready to attack. Upon this the Australians opened fire on a party of stretcher-bearers who were still wandering about in the failing light. At once the Turkish artillery started up again and the bombardment continued intermittently all night.

Hamilton says he was very much annoyed when he heard of these irregular dealings with the enemy, and he dispatched Braithwaite to Anzac to handle the negotiations. The following letter, addressed to '*Commandant en chef des Forces Britanniques, Sir John Hamilton*,' arrived from Liman von Sanders.

> *Grand Quartier Général de la 5 me. Armée Ottomane.*
> *le 22 mai 1915.*
> *Excellence,*
> *J'ai l'honneur d'informer Votre Excellence que les propositions concernant la conclusion d'un armistice pour enterrer les morts et secourir les blessés des deux parties adverses, ont trouvé mon plein consentement – et que seuls nos sentiments d'humanité nous y ont déterminés.*
> *J'ai investi le lieutenant-colonel Fahreddin du pouvoir de signer en mon nom.*
> *J'ai l'honneur d'être avec assurance de ma plus haute considération.*
>
> > *Liman von Sanders,*
> > *Commandant en chef de la 5 me. Armée Ottomane.*

Translated, this reads:

> Your Excellency,
> I have the honour to inform your Excellency that the proposal for the conclusion of an armistice to bury the dead and rescue the wounded of both combatants has met with my full agreement – and that only feelings of humanity have influenced us.
> I have authorised Lt. Col. Fahreddin with authority to sign on my behalf.
> I have the honour to assure you of my great esteem.

There is an air of fantasy about the conference that took

place at Birdwood's headquarters on 22 May. Herbert walked through heavy showers of rain along the Gaba Tepe beach, and a 'fierce Arab officer and a wandery-looking Turkish lieutenant' came out to meet him. They sat down and smoked in a field of scarlet poppies. Presently Kemal himself arrived on horseback with other Turkish officers, and they were blind-folded and led on foot into the Anzac bridgehead. The British intelligence officers were anxious to give the impression that a great deal of barbed-wire entanglement had been erected on the beach, and they forced Kemal to keep goose-stepping over imaginary obstacles as he went along. Presently the Turks were remounted and taken to Birdwood's dugout by the beach.

The conference in the narrow cave was a stiff and strained affair, the Turkish Beys in their gold lace, the British generals in their red tabs, each side trying to make it clear that it was not they who were eager for the armistice. But the atmosphere was relieved by one moment of pure farce: an Australian soldier, not knowing or caring about what was going on inside the dugout, put his head round the canvas flap and demanded, 'Have any of you bastards got my kettle?'

Herbert meanwhile had been taken into the Turkish lines as a hostage. He was mounted on a horse and blindfolded, and then led round and round in circles to confuse his sense of direction. At one stage the fierce Arab officer cried out to the man who was supposed to be leading the horse, 'You old fool. Can't you see he's riding straight over the cliff?' Herbert protested strongly and they went on again. When finally the bandage was taken from his eyes he found himself in a tent in a grove of olives, and the Arab officer said, 'This is the beginning of a lifelong friendship'. He ordered cheese, tea and coffee to be brought, and offered to eat first to prove that the food was not poisoned. They had an amiable conversation, and in the evening when Kemal and the other Turks came back from Birdwood's head-quarters Herbert was blindfolded again and returned to the British lines.

The terms of the truce had been settled as precisely as possible; it was to take place on 24 May and was to continue for nine hours. Three zones were to be marked out with white flags for the burial of the dead – one Turkish, one British and the third common to both sides. Priests, doctors and soldiers taking part in the burials were to wear white armbands and were not to use field-glasses or enter enemy trenches. All firing was of course to cease along the line, and the soldiers in the opposing trenches were not to put their heads above their parapets during the period of the truce. It was also agreed that all rifles minus their bolts were to be handed back to whichever side they belonged to – but this move was circumvented to some extent by the Australians, who on the previous evening crept out into no-man's-land and gathered up as many weapons as they could find.

The morning of 24 May broke wet and cold, and the soldiers were in their greatcoats. Soon after dawn the firing died away, and at six-thirty Herbert set out again with a group of officers for Gaba Tepe beach. Heavy rain was falling. After an hour the Turks arrived – Herbert's acquaintance of two days before and several others, including a certain Arif, the son of Achmet Pasha, who handed Herbert a visiting card inscribed with the words, *Sculpteur et Peintre. Etudiant de Poésie*.

Together the two parties left the beach, and passing through cornfields flecked with poppies walked up to the hills where the battle had taken place.

Many of the dead had sunk to the ground in the precise attitude they had adopted at the moment when the bullets stopped their rush, their hands clasping their bayonets, their heads thrust forward or doubled up beneath them. Nothing was missing except the spark of life. They lay in mounds on the wet earth, whole companies of soldiers, like some ghastly tableau made of wax.

Among the living men there was at first some little friction. Everyone was nervous, everyone expected that even in these awful nightmarish surroundings some kind of treachery had been planned by the other side. There were complaints: the Australians were stealing arms: the Turks were coming too close to the Anzac trenches. At Quinn's Post, where the lines were only ten or fifteen yards apart, the tension was almost a palpable thing in the air, an inflammable essence that might explode at any moment. Hands on their triggers, the men watched one another across the narrow space, expecting at every minute that someone would make some foolish gesture that would start the fighting again. On the wider stretches of the battlefield, however, Turks and Anzac troops worked together in digging great communal graves, and as the hours went by they began to fraternise, offering cigarettes to one another, talking in broken scraps of English and Arabic, exchanging badges and gadgets from their pockets as souvenirs.

Herbert was kept busy settling points of difference. He allowed the Turks to extract for burial some bodies which had been built into their emplacements, and once he was even permitted to go into the enemy trenches to satisfy himself that the Turks were not using this lull to fortify and advance their positions. He found there a group of soldiers whom he had known previously in Albania. They gathered round him cheering and clapping, and he had to stop them because they were interrupting the burial services which were being conducted round about by the Moslem Imams and the Christian priests. From this time onwards the Turks were constantly coming up to him for orders, and even getting him to sign receipts for money taken from the dead. Intervals of bright sunshine had now followed the rain.

Compton Mackenzie and Major Jack Churchill (the brother of Winston Churchill) had come over from the *Arcadian* for the day, and they stood on a parapet constructed chiefly of dead bodies to watch the scene. 'In the foreground,' Mackenzie writes, 'was a narrow stretch of level scrub along which white flags were stuck at intervals, and a line of sentries, Australians and Turks, faced one another. Staff officers of both sides were standing around in little groups, and there was an atmosphere about the scene of local magnates at the annual sports making suggestions about the start of the obstacle race. Aubrey Herbert looked so like the indispensable bachelor that every country neighbourhood retains to take complete control of the proceedings on such occasions. Here he was, shuffling about, loose-gaited, his neck out-thrust and swinging from side to side as he went peering up into people's faces to see whether they were the enemy or not, so that, if they were, he could offer them cigarettes and exchange a few courtesies with them in their own language. . . .

'The impression which that scene from the ridge by Quinn's Post made on my mind has obliterated all the rest of the time at Anzac. I cannot recall a single incident on the way back down the valley. I know only that nothing could cleanse the smell of death from the nostrils for a fortnight afterwards. There was no herb so aromatic but it reeked of carrion, not thyme nor lavender, nor even rosemary.'

By three in the afternoon the work was practically done. There were two crises: it was discovered at the last minute that the Turks' watches were eight minutes ahead of the British, and a hurried adjustment had to be made. Then, as the hour for the ending of the truce was approaching, a shot rang out. Standing there in the open with tens of thousands of rifles pointed towards them the burial parties stood in a sudden hush, but nothing followed and they returned to their work again.

At four o'clock the Turks near Quinn's Post came to Herbert for their final orders, since none of their own officers were about. He first sent back the gravediggers to their own trenches, and at seven minutes past four retired the men who were carrying the white flags. He then walked over to the Turkish trenches to say goodbye. When he remarked to the enemy soldiers there that they would probably shoot him on the following day, they answered in a horrified chorus, 'God forbid.' See Herbert standing there, groups of Australians came up to the Turks to shake hands and say goodbye, 'Goodbye, old chap; good luck.' The Turks answered with one of their proverbs: 'Smiling may you go and smiling may you come again.'

All the remaining men in the open were now sent back to their lines, and Herbert made a last minute inspection along the front, reminding the Turks that firing was not to begin again for a further twenty-five minutes. He was answered with salaams, and he too finally dropped out of sight. At 4.45 p.m. a Turkish sniper fired from somewhere in the hills. Immediately the Australians answered and the roar of high explosive closed over the battlefield again.

Despite almost incessant attacks by a numerically superior enemy, the toll of disease, lack of food and water, and as the misery of summer's extreme heat changed to winter, floods, intense cold and lack of proper clothing, the Anzac troops held on for a further seven months, periodically attacking and inflicting heavy casualties on the enemy. They were never defeated.

But the failure all along the coastline to drive out the Turks made withdrawal inevitable. It was the sole tactical triumph of the British command. Between 10 December and 9 January all the troops were safely evacuated. The men at Anzac Cove and nearby Suvla Bay began leaving each night after 12 December. In six days 40 000 men with most of their equipment moved in secret to the barges and ferries. At the peak of the evacuation, on 19 December, 20 000 men got away without the enemy being aware of it.

Nearly half a million British, Australian, New Zealand and French troops fought at Gallipoli; 252 000 were casualties. The Turkish figures for men engaged in the fighting and the casualties were almost identical to those of their adversaries. Also shared by both sides was the outstanding courage shown in the face of a battle neither could win.

Notes

[1] Or 'Eggs-a-cook', an expression used by the Egyptian vendors when they sold eggs to the Anzac troops during their stay in Egypt.
[2] The island base from which the invasion fleet sailed. The armistice with the Allies was signed by the Turks on the island on 30 October, 1918.

THE FIRST TANK BATTLE

The development of the tank by Britain was one of the best-kept secrets of the First World War. Largely as the result of the insistence of Winston Churchill, then First Lord of the Admiralty, the design and testing of a tracked armoured vehicle began in 1915. Because of the Navy's interest in the project the first tanks were officially classified as His Majesty's Land Ships, the description soon being changed for reasons of security to cistern, container, or tank on the theory that the names would satisfy the curious who saw the bulky vehicle under covers in factory yards or on testing grounds. The men manning the first satisfactory tank, *Big Willie*, were enlisted as personnel of the Heavy Section, Machine Gun Corps. In the late summer of 1916, the first tanks were transported in great secrecy to France, and on 15 September they were ready to join General Henry Rawlinson's Fourth Army in a new phase of the Battle of the Somme, where the British forces had suffered 60 000 casualties on the first day and the carnage had continued week after week.

The Battle of the Somme had been in progress for nearly ten weeks when the officers and men of the Heavy Section arrived with their tanks at that sector of the front where the Fourth Army, by means of a surprise night attack in mid-July, had managed to advance and occupy four miles of devastated country. Most of them had never been to the Western Front before. They found themselves in a strange world in which endless lines of transport crawled over incredibly bad roads bordered by jagged stumps of trees and a tragic litter of dead men and horses and rotting equipment. The Germans were counter-attacking over the whole thirty-mile front and guns sounded everywhere.

During the nights of 13 and 14 September the tanks, which had been camouflaged, were moved up to the assembly area under a cloak of great secrecy. Driving at night through the mud and in and out of shell holes was extremely difficult, even though white tapes had been laid on the ground for the commanders who were guiding the vehicles by walking in front, and a number broke down or became irretrievably ditched. Of the forty-eight tanks allocated to the battle, only thirty-two reached their starting positions in the front line. One tank commander reported that his driver baulked at going down a narrow sunken road strewn with dead bodies.

Equipping the tanks for battle order had been a major problem. Every crew member, the officer and seven men, carried two gas helmets, one pair of goggles, and a leather 'antibruise' helmet in addition to his ordinary service cap and the usual equipment consisting of a revolver, haversack, first aid kit, water bottle and iron rations. All this was dumped on the floor as the crew came aboard. But there was much more. Each tank carried thirty tins of food, sixteen loaves, cheese, tea, sugar and milk; drums of engine oil and grease; a spare Vickers machine gun and four replacement barrels, together with 33 000 rounds of ammunition; water-cans, boxes of revolver ammunition, wire cutters, and many other items. A difficult problem still unresolved had been providing a means of communication between tanks in battle and between tanks and the infantry with whom they were operating. A crude wireless transmitter had been designed and fitted into each tank with 100 yards of cable, attached to a second instrument which was to be left at the jumping off place. The cable was to be unwound as the tank advanced and messages relayed to a wireless operator behind. What happened when the tank advanced further was not explained. In any event the device was not used since nothing could be heard above the noise of the engine. Communication between tanks was carried out by displaying metal discs, by semaphore with metal arms, and by morse flag signalling out of the roof manhole. (One officer plaintively recalled that the three flags provided for this purpose were often lost amongst the stores just when they were most needed.) Many tanks carried a more reliable means of communication in the form of two carrier pigeons, the idea being to release them when main objectives were reached so that the battle commander could be informed of progress. The tank commanders were supplied with rice paper on which messages were to be written in code and put into metal tubes attached to the pigeons' legs. (It was not unknown, however, for a tank commander to forget to send these messages in the heat of battle and to choose pigeon pie as one way of destroying the evidence.)

Three days of intensive artillery bombardment preceded the attack, whose objective was to break through the German lines to the important road centre of Bapaume and make way for the cavalry to dash forward and roll up the enemy front northward, as intended in the original plan of 1 July. Ten tanks were to work with the Guards Division and six with the 6th and 56th Divisions on the right, their objectives being Ginchy and the Quadrilateral, while on the left of the front eight tanks were allotted to the III Corps, attacking through High Wood and east of Martinpuich, and eighteen to the XV Corps. The remaining six were attached to the Reserve Army, the 5th Canadian Corps, which was to attack between Pozières and Martinpuich.

The morning of the 15th was fine with a thin ground mist. Although the main attack was not to begin until 6.20 a.m., behind a creeping artillery barrage, the battle was opened one hour earlier by the advance of a solitary tank in a preliminary operation to drive the enemy out of a pocket just ahead of the British front near Delville Wood. This was D 1, under the command of Captain H. W. Mortimore. Two other tanks were also to have been used but one had broken down and the other was ditched. The effect on the Germans, who had never seen such a vehicle before, was electrifying. As the tank crawled towards them out of the mist, shells firing from the bulbous sponsons on either side and a machine-gun spitting from the front turret, many of them fled in terror. The pocket was quickly cleared for the infantry following a quarter of an hour later.

This reaction to the first appearance of tanks was repeated on all parts of the front where they were used, giving some indication of the effect that a massed attack by several hundred tanks would have achieved. The following description was written by a German newspaper correspondent who witnessed the first ever tank attack:

'When the German outposts crept out of their dugouts in the mist of the morning and stretched their necks to look for the English, their blood was chilled in their veins. Mysterious monsters were crawling towards them over the craters. Stunned as if an earthquake had burst around them, they all rubbed their eyes, fascinated by the fabulous creatures.

'Their imaginations were still excited by the effects of the artillery bombardment. It was no wonder then that imagination got the better of these sorely tried men, who knew well enough that the enemy would try every means to destroy our steel wall of fragile human bodies. These men no longer knew what fear is. But here was some devilry which the brain of man had invented, with powerful mechanical forces, a mystery which rooted one to the ground because the intelligence could not grasp it, a fate before which one felt helpless.

'One stared and stared as if one had lost the power of one's limbs. The monsters approached slowly, hobbling, rolling and rocking, but they approached. Nothing impeded them; a supernatural force seemed to impel them on. Someone in the trenches said "the devil is coming", and the word was passed along the line like wildfire.

'Suddenly tongues of flame leapt out of the armoured sides of the iron caterpillars. Shells whistled over our heads and the sound of machine gun fire filled the air. The mysterious creature had yielded its secret as the English infantry rolled up in waves behind the "devil's coaches".'

One of the men to go into this first tank battle, William Divall, later described the experience in a letter to his sister:

'As the tanks travel over the front trench, the troops rub their eyes in wonder at their strange, cube-impressionist coats of many colours. The deck of the tank rolls and pitches like a torpedo boat in a storm. But we are all old hands – ABs in fact – and we come safely through without seasickness.

'Hun bullets are rebounding from our tough sides like hail from a glass roof. We just crawl over the embankment, guns and all. It is not necessary to fire a single shot. Two or three Huns are brave enough to creep on the back of the tank from behind. We open a small trapdoor and shoot them with a revolver.

'It is almost like playing hide-and-seek as we travel backward and forward along the trench.

'Inside the tank is the crew, strangely garbed, as becomes their strange craft, while around them is a complicated mass of machinery. We succeed in putting out two machine gun emplacements, the guns of which have been worrying our infantry for some time. And now the action begins in earnest. The whole crew are at various guns, which break forth in a devastating fire.

'By this time the fumes from hundreds of rounds which we have fired, with the heat from the engines and the waste petrol and oil, have made the air quite oppressive and uncomfortable to breathe. However, those who go down to the land in tanks are accustomed to many strange sensations, which would make an ordinary mortal shudder.

'We make a fairly difficult target as our way lies between numerous tree trunks and battered stumps, also much barbed wire. We are battling bravely with the waves of earth we encounter. But thanks to our protective headgear, we come through it all.

'The last trench proves to be the worst, for just as we are crossing a large hole, our bus stops. I believe the sparking plugs have ceased to sparkle, and it is a very awkward place as the tree stumps now prevent free traverse of our guns. . . .

'And now the old bus is going strong again. Only just in time for a large lyddite bomb bursts against the armoured jacket of my gun. The flare comes in through the port-hole, blinding me for a minute or so, while splinters strike my face. But my gun is still untouched, thanks to the armourplate, and somehow seems to work much better.

'The Germans are now scattered in small parties. After a few short runs we find no more Huns to hunt, so as our objective, the wood, has been gained, we leave the scene to the infantry and find shelter from possible stray shells in a large hole which has been made by many shells.

'After a little exercise we start to overhaul the tanks and guns, in readiness for the next joy ride. Then we snatch a few hours of sleep.'

Of the thirty-two tanks which left their starting positions, nine broke down from mechanical trouble and five became ditched. The remaining eighteen met with varying success but the greatest achievement of the day was the assault on the village of Flers, nearly a mile forward. Seven tanks of D Company led the attack by a New Zealand and an English division in the centre of the XV Corps sector. Four were knocked out by direct hits, but by 8.40 a.m. three had managed to push on to the outskirts of the village, smashing machine-gun posts, breaking down fortified houses, and spreading so much panic among the enemy that most of them fled back along the road to Gueudecourt. D 17 (*Dinnaken*), commanded by Captain Hastie, drove right through the village, followed by parties of infantry who were braced for the usual ordeal of house-to-house fighting, only to find that the enemy had been cleared out by the tanks. They did not suffer a single casualty. It was the furthest penetration achieved by any tank that day and, as it happened, was witnessed by an observer in a British aircraft overhead who sent back a message that was to be widely reported in the British Press: 'A tank is walking up the High Street of Flers with the British Army cheering behind.'

The spectacular success of the tank was all too brief, due to the lack of replacements and reinforcements. The Battle of the Somme continued until the end of November, the Allied armies gaining a few kilometres of ground but with the German defences unbroken. The casualties on both sides exceeded a million. Belatedly the futility of pitting men and cavalry against massed artillery and machine guns was accepted. The C-in-C Field Marshal Douglas Haig asked that 1000 tanks be built immediately, commenting that on the Somme 'wherever the tanks advanced we took our objectives and where they did not advance we failed to take our objectives'. In the final weeks of the war in the autumn of 1918 some 2000 tanks and armoured vehicles formed the spearhead in storming the German defences and breaking through the 'impregnable' Hindenburg Line; and the German Supreme Command began negotiations for an Armistice.

BATTLE OF THE RIVER PLATE

COURSE OF
GRAF SPEE

SHIPS SUNK
BY GRAF SPEE

Thirteen days before Britain formally declared war on
Germany on 3 September, 1939, the pocket battleship
Admiral Graf Spee, armed with six 11-inch guns and
eight 5.9-inch guns, sailed from her home base at
Wilhelmshaven, bound for the North Atlantic. By the
time hostilities broke out this commerce raider had
moved undetected to the South Atlantic. She made her
first kill on 30 September when she sank an ocean tramp
off the coast of Brazil. News that one of the most powerful battleships in the world was loose in the Atlantic
resulted in the Admiralty organising eight hunting
groups, comprising every available battleship, cruiser
and carrier in the Royal Navy and the French Navy.
They began searching more than 24 million square miles
of ocean.

In October the *Graf Spee* sank four merchant ships in
the South Atlantic. Rounding the Cape of Good Hope,

she ranged the Indian Ocean long enough to sink two more, and then returned to the South Atlantic with two more kills in November. The Admiralty calculated that the *Graf Spee*'s commander, Captain Hans Langsdorff, would move towards the South American coast to attack ships carrying meat and wheat from Argentine and Uruguay ports at the mouth of the River Plate.

On 12 December Royal Navy Force G, with three fast cruisers, *Exeter*, *Ajax* and *Achilles*, under the command of Commodore Henry Harwood, sailed to an area 240 km east of the South American coast and in the shipping lane. Somewhere farther east was the *Graf Spee*.

December 13 dawned clear and sunny as the three cruisers of Force G patrolled in line ahead through the flat calm. Visibility was near perfect when at 6.14 a.m. a look-out in *Ajax* sighted a smudge far away on the north-western horizon. *Exeter* raced ahead to investigate and two minutes later her signal light flashed back to *Ajax*, 'I think it is a pocket battleship'. Harwood immediately ordered full speed and his ships deployed quickly into their pre-arranged positions as gun crews rushed headlong to their turrets.

There was much less sense of urgency aboard the *Graf Spee*. Her spotter plane was out of action and the look-outs had made out the *Exeter*; the four tiny masts coming up behind her were believed to be screening destroyers. Confident that his radar-controlled main armament could make short work of a single cruiser, Langsdorff decided to close rapidly for a quick kill. This misjudgement cost Langsdorff his principal advantage of being able to out-range, as well as out-gun, the enemy cruiser. This would have frustrated Commodore Harwood's tactical plan to use his weaker squadron's superior speed to divide the pocket battleship's fire.

At 6.18 a.m. the first salvo thundered from *Graf Spee*'s

forward turret, as Langsdorff concentrated his fire on the bigger cruiser with occasional shots at the lighter ships. Two minutes later HMS *Exeter* fired back, soon followed by *Ajax* and *Achilles*. Six minutes after opening fire, one of *Graf Spee*'s 11-in shells had wrecked *Exeter*'s 'B' turret and swept the bridge with a murderous hail of splinters. Everyone was killed or badly injured except Captain Bell who made his way through the wreckage and fires to con the ship from the emergency steering position aft. To gain some relief from the severe hammering his ship was taking, he ordered the firing of the starboard torpedoes which forced the pocket battleship temporarily to turn away.

Just before Harwood's flagship, *Ajax*, had joined the action, she had catapulted her light aircraft to spot for gunnery control but the action soon became so confused that differentiating between the fall of shot from the three British ships became impossible and gunnery accuracy worsened as the range opened up. Now Langsdorff saw his chance to concentrate all his firepower on the *Exeter* and he closed for the kill. But Harwood's two light cruisers, racing in with every gun blazing away, put up such a spirited attack that the pocket battleship turned to deal with her new assailants. This bold stratagem gave Captain Bell enough time to haul *Exeter* away as his last turret was put out of action. Blazing furiously amidships, the badly battered cruiser withdrew from the action.

With *Graf Spee* now turning every gun on to the light cruisers, the captains of *Ajax* and *Achilles* found their ship handling tested to its limit as they weaved at high speed to dodge the German salvoes which surrounded them with giant waterspouts. Luck was on their side, until two of *Ajax*'s turrets were knocked out in quick succession and her mast was brought down by another well-placed salvo. The action had now become too hot and Harwood, knowing that his lightly-armoured cruisers would not take much more punishment, ordered torpedoes to be fired and the range to be opened under cover of a smokescreen.

When the *Graf Spee* turned away to avoid their

torpedoes, the action, which had lasted for a furious ninety minutes, subsided shortly after 7.30 a.m.

Casualties had been heavy in the crippled *Exeter*, with sixty-four of her officers and men killed. She was now heading towards the Falkland Islands naval base as damage control parties battled with the fires that threatened to overwhelm her. *Ajax*, with two of her turrets out of action and seven men dead, together with the less badly damaged *Achilles*, had taken up station astern of the pocket battleship, just beyond gun range. The *Graf Spee*'s fighting ability was still unimpaired although she had suffered twenty hits and thirty-six men were dead. Most of the light cruisers' 6-in shells had bounced off her armoured sides but her superstructure was battered, her bakery was wrecked and an 8-in shell from *Exeter* had torn a six-foot hole above the waterline. Instead of turning on his pursuers, Langsdorff decided to make for the shelter of Montevideo, the nearest neutral port, to patch up the damage.

The *Graf Spee* anchored just before midnight in the harbour and for the next four days the Uruguayan capital was the scene of intense diplomatic activity. The German Ambassador argued for, and was granted, an extension to the twenty-four hours for repairs allowed under international law whilst the British sought to delay her sailing so that the battlecruiser *Renown* and carrier *Ark Royal*, then refuelling north of Rio de Janeiro, could join up with the two light cruisers off the Plate. A succession of British cargo ships sailed daily to prevent the warship leaving until the regulatory twenty-four hours which had to elapse after every such departure. All light aircraft that could have flown reconnaissance missions became 'unavailable' to the Germans and the BBC overseas broadcasts reinforced the carefully laid rumours that a battleship and aircraft carriers had arrived off the Plate. All these developments were anxiously watched by the United States Government, fearing that another naval battle would make a nonsense of their Neutrality Zone warnings.

On 16 December with the seventy-two hour extension

running out, Langsdorff telegraphed Raeder[1] for instructions, reporting that strong British forces made 'a breakthrough to home waters hopeless'. He proposed battling his way across the muddy river to the sympathetic neutrality of Buenos Aires. If this proved impossible, he asked for a decision on whether the ship should be scuttled or interned. The Führer was consulted, and making clear his displeasure over the whole situation, instructed Raeder to signal back: '*NO* internment in Uruguay. Attempt effective destruction if ship is scuttled.'

At 6.15 p.m. on 17 December 1939, the *Graf Spee* moved slowly out of Montevideo harbour with her battle ensigns flying. Further down the wide Plate estuary the *Ajax* and *Achilles*, which had been reinforced by the heavy cruiser *Cumberland*, closed up to action stations. Crowds lined the waterfront expecting the opening shots in a dramatic battle. Then, to everybody's astonishment, the pocket battleship stopped just outside the three-mile limit and through binoculars they saw her skeleton crew being transferred to the German freighter alongside. Minutes later, just as the first red glow of sunset began to stain the muddy water, explosions erupted throughout the warship. The Wagnerian spectacle brought to an end the *Graf Spee*'s career in which she had sunk 50 000 tons of merchant shipping and tied down half of the British Fleet. Throughout the night sheets of flame licked round her blackened hulk as she settled on the river bed. Langsdorff, after reaching the safety of pro-German Argentina, wrote a final testament two days later. It concluded: 'I am quite happy to pay with my life for any possible reflection on the honour of the flag.' That night he shot himself, after he had carefully wrapped himself in the Imperial Navy Ensign under which he had fought at Jutland.

The battle of the River Plate was the first Allied major naval victory of the Second World War, and a much needed fillip for Britain at a time when magnetic mines and U-boat attacks were sinking so many merchant ships that food stocks had dropped to a crisis level. In Winston Churchill's words, 'in a cold winter it warmed the cockles of the British nation's heart.'

Commodore Harwood was knighted and promoted to Rear Admiral. Due respect was paid by his adversaries to Captain Langsdorff as a resourceful and chivalrous seaman. During the brief operation of the *Graf Spee* more than 360 British merchant seamen, picked up from the sunken ships, were treated with courtesy and consideration. Sixty-two were on board during the battle and were put ashore when the *Graf Spee* limped into Montevideo. Very different treatment was experienced by the merchant seamen who had been transferred to the *Graf Spee*'s supply ship, the *Altmark*, some time before the battle. They were brutally treated during the long voyage while the *Altmark* eluded attack and reached a Norwegian fjord in February. There HMS *Cossack* put a rescue party on board the *Altmark*, the Navy men bursting into the hold with the now famous cry 'the Navy's here', one of the most dramatic rescues in the history of sea warfare.

Note

[1] Admiral Erich Raeder, Commander-in-Chief of the Kriegsmarine (Germany's Navy).

ONE OF THE FEW

As the overture for Operation Sealion, Germany's plan for the invasion of Britain in 1940, Herman Goering, commander-in-chief of the Luftwaffe, assured Hitler that his bombers and fighters would destroy all resistance by the RAF, thus enabling the landings on the south and south-eastern coast of England to proceed without attack from the air.

The first dog fights in the Battle of Britain began on 2 July, steadily increasing until on 13 August the full strength of the Luftwaffe was hurled across the Channel. Swarms of fighters escorted the bomber squadrons, but they could not fight off the attacking RAF fighters for more than twenty or thirty minutes if they were to get back to their bases in France before fuel was exhausted. But the British defenders were battling over their own country, and could quickly find an airfield. Even if an aircraft was damaged or destroyed the pilot had a fair chance of parachuting to safety, eager to fight again.

Because of the need to utilise the advantage of tides and moonlight invasion day had to be on 27 September or a day or two later. This meant that irreversible preparations of armour, troops and all the material for a vicious war had to start on 17 September, with Goering's promise of a RAF mortally injured by then a reality. Angrily determined to have his day of triumph and disprove the doubts of the German army and naval commanders, he ordered a ruthless series of mass attacks on 15 September.

This is the story of one RAF fighter pilot on that historic Sunday in 1940, now rightly celebrated as Battle of Britain Day. Sergeant James ('Ginger') Lacey was twenty-three years old. He had learned to fly before he was twenty. During the Nazi blitzkrieg on France he shot down five enemy aircraft. Returning with his squadron – No. 501 (City of Gloucester) – to Kenley airfield after Dunkerque, Lacey was soon battling with enemy raiders. On 13 September he was shot down, parachuting from his blazing aircraft to safety, but with burns on his legs. He concealed his injuries so that the medical officer would not ground him. On the evening of 14 September he went to bed, knowing that the next day would be straining Britain's defences to the limit. He left an order to be called at 4.30 a.m.

In the east the sky was whitening, the light colouring the field's grass green and the virginia creeper on the old houses red. The still forms of three-bladed grey-green Hurricanes on the field's western edge, each with a battery cart beside it, emerged clearly out of the fading darkness. Lacey walked out to one of the nearest low-wing fighters. On the fuselage above the big belly air scoop were painted the letters SD, four feet high. Just behind the squadron letters, farther back on the fuselage, was a smaller F. (Lacey refused to have the F painted on after having been shot down on several occasions the day after it had been painted. It was chalked on.)

He greeted fitter and rigger, carefully laid his parachute on the tail elevator, straps properly arranged for the critical moment later when he would be dashing out from the dispersal hut. He climbed in the cockpit and checked the length of the rudder bar (adjusted by turning a spider wheel between the pedals). He set the tail elevator trim for take-off and opened the trap door on the gunsight directly in front to see if an extra bulb was in the clip. The little white bulbs which produced the light ring on the gunsight glass, all-important in combat, were scarce, and Lacey not only checked on the sight bulb and spare each morning but usually carried extras in his pocket. Bulbs in place, he hung his helmet on the right side of the gunsight and pushed the nozzle of the black rubber hose which protruded from it into the oxygen outlet, turning the nozzle to lock it in place. He plugged the lead wire from his helmet into a radio wire connection on the right-hand side of the cockpit floor. (It had a habit of coming out at embarrassing moments, causing loss of radio contact.) Then he signed form 700, the serviceability log, which, in effect, said he was satisfied that the aircraft was fit to fly. Fitter and rigger signed before him.

There was no activity yet, and satisfied all was in order, Lacey chatted leisurely with crewmen about the night before – invariably the first topic of the morning. The sky was now fully lighted and he walked back to the dispersal hut. Pilots who were scheduled to fly, and some who were not, tried to relax; those not scheduled were noticeably more successful, many sleeping soundly. Lacey sank into a chair and tried to sleep but couldn't. The minutes passed, then an hour and then another. The morning was wearing on; the time came for tea-break. So far, 15 September had been an easy day.

The waiting resumes after the break. Clouds are beginning to drift in above the field, which takes some of the sting out of the sun's rays as they beat down on Lacey's fair and, in some places burned, skin. Minutes tick by and the clock moves from 11.30 past the half-hour. Over-casual glances and subdued tension are noticeable in the hut.

The telephone! Someone near the table picks up the receiver. All eyes focus on his every move. He is motioning pilots up. Scramble! Everyone is instantly in motion. Lacey bolts through the door shouting, 'Start up!' His fitter, a short distance away, leaps into the cockpit while the rigger runs to the battery cart. Crewmen at the other Hurricanes are also in action. Pilots don't know yet what enemy force they're scrambling to meet – they'll learn details by radio.

Lacey runs up just as the big Rolls-Merlin is coughing to a start, smoke belching from its exhausts, propeller spinning. He grabs his chute, catches the half belt to his left at the safety box and holds the box to his stomach as he fits in the shoulder- and leg-straps and closes the catch. He jumps on the port wing as the fitter scrambles out on the starboard, and into the cockpit, pulling on his helmet as the fitter quickly lays the straps over his shoulders. He fits them and side-straps over the peg, fits in the pin. Now ready, he casts a glance right towards Squadron Leader Hogan's Hurricane. Hogan is ready. Lacey's fitter taps his right shoulder – he always does – shouts, 'Good Luck' and jumps off the wing. Hogan's fighter is taxi-ing out; Lacey pushes the throttle knob forward with his left hand, releases brakes, and amid the roar of the engine and wind the Hurricane begins to roll. Their clothes flapping in the propwash, fitter and rigger watch as the thundering fighter moves away, gathering speed. Lacey taxies into position on Hogan's wing, and Hogan now applies full throttle. The fighters are taking off straight ahead and Lacey keeps his eyes on Hogan, about thirty feet ahead and right. He checks gauges in quick snatches ... engine temperature, revolutions, oil pressure, boost, radiator shutter lever back ... all in order. The Hurricane bounds forward and the Merlin's power pulls it faster and faster. The bumps are lighter ... the wheels are off the ground. Lacey holds the stick back. He eases back a bit on boost (to avoid overstrain). The Squadron Leader's vic and Pinetree Red Three[1] are airborne.

The three Hurricanes lean into a slight turn, lifting away from the field. Lacey retracts his undercarriage, flips the red handle on the right of the instrument panel, raising the flaps, and pushes back the black knob on the cockpit floor to close the coolant shutters – never taking his eyes off Hogan for more than a second. He and Red Two are very close to Hogan; the other three vics, as they lift off, cut off the Squadron Leader in tighter turns and soon the two-flight squadron is tucked in neatly and climbing. Over the earphones comes Hogan's voice: 'Check in, Red Section.' 'Red Two,' a voice replies. 'Red Three', Lacey transmits. Then each pilot in the squadron checks in, in yellow, green and blue vics.

Now the vital information comes in over the earphones from the controller below: 'Pinetree Leader, vector one-three-zero, repeat one-three-zero. Angels fifteen[2]. We have fifty-plus raid for you, approaching between Dungeness and Ramsgate.' Hogan acknowledges and a ripple of excitement permeates the squadron as it slants upwards into a partly cloudy south-eastern sky.

Lacey flips the gunsight switch; an orange circle appears in the middle of the sighting glass, which represents 100 mph in deflection shots (a two-circle lead for an aircraft flying perpendicularly at 200 mph). The space between the two bars on the glass can be widened or closed by adjusting the wing-span setter. An aircraft is within range from behind when the wing-tips touch the bars on each side. Lacey has had his eight .303 Browning machine-guns harmonised for convergence at 150 yards, 100 yards closer than the normal firing pattern. His gun-belts are loaded with his own selection of ammunition: one De Wilde armour-piercing incendiary for every standard, the normal proportion being one to five. The De Wilde is what his armourer, Sergeant 'Dapper' Green, calls a 'dirty' loading. It has a tendency to foul the gun barrels but Lacey doesn't care whether barrels are fouled or not. Green, an admirer, reluctantly supplies the extra De Wilde ammunition – and almost weeps when he sees the guns after each combat.

The fighters reach higher and higher. The enemy will be high . . . controller directed Hogan to angels fifteen, which sounds like 15 000 feet — but 'fifteen' is a code word meaning 25 000. (Ten is automatically added to the controller's instruction.) The hope is to conceal from the Germans, who are often successful at monitoring RAF radio conversations, how high RAF fighters will be. If the Hurricanes surprise the faster enemy fighters from above, it is a considerable tactical advantage. But that is not easy to do from a scramble. The 109 has both a higher ceiling and a speed advantage.[3]

Every pilot scans the sky ahead and above for the enemy gaggle as the Rolls-Merlins thrust the hump-backed RAF fighters upwards at almost 200 mph. The Hurricane, with its low wing loading of 27 pounds per square foot, out-climbs its RAF partner, the Spitfire, which is otherwise the faster of the two.   The Hurricane can also take more punishment. It has a top speed of about 330 (compared to the Spit's 367). Lacey is not envious of his comrades flying Spits, whom he refers to as 'glamour-boys'.

The squadron reaches 8000 feet, 9000, 10 000, course south-east. Ashford is in view below. The enemy should appear at any moment. The squadron obviously won't reach 25 000 before interception. Now the controller calls Hogan: bandits straight ahead, above! Lacey sweeps the sky ahead, sees nothing. Each pilot, silently and tensely searches the sky, listening, checking his sight and guns. Altitude reaches 12 000 feet, 13 000, 14 000, the squadron still at maximum climb. Below it's close to lunchtime on the pleasant summer terraces of Kent and Sussex gardens.

'Bogies, twelve o'clock high!' The shout acts as an electric shock. 'Tally-ho,' Hogan responds. Lacey fixes his eyes ahead, and above . . . there they are . . . a big gaggle . . . 2000 feet above, ahead. The enemy has the height advantage.

The dark shapes become larger by the second. Lacey's eyes stay on them. What aircraft? He sees two-engined bombers and also smaller shapes. Me.109s! Hogan pulls up towards them to make a head-on pass. Lacey pulls back on the spade-handle stick, forcing the nose of his Hurricane up. The whole squadron steepens its climb, but Lacey climbs more steeply than the rest and his speed slackens. The silhouettes of the German aircraft grow wider and they come on, above. The bombers – much larger – are Do.17s.[4] The two forces are closing fast. Lacey realises they'll pass too far overhead. Hogan can't get the squadron up high enough for a head-on pass! Desperate, Lacey pulls the stick handle back and the Hurricane climbs higher but airspeed slips. The Do.17s and Me.109s come on. The straining RAF interceptors will miss them! The two formations flash together at 400 mph. But the Germans are a thousand feet higher. Lacey's Hurricane almost stands on its tail. His eyes are locked on one of the Do.17s. Sighting almost straight up through the glass, as the enemy sweeps over above, he pulls the Hurricane straight up. Range 1200 feet. Too far? His thumb presses the silver gun button. The eight Brownings roar. But the recoil and the angle of flight exert themselves. The Hurricane shudders. Lacey tries to dip the stick, recover. No response. He's lost flying speed, the nose won't dip. He stalls, falls off out of control to the right, into a spin.

Plunging towards the ground, he must forget the enemy and regain control. Momentarily thrown about the cockpit by violent buffeting and turning, he begins the all-important recovery procedure. Stick forward . . . let her dive . . . opposite rudder. Speed increases, the buffeting eases. The fighter straightens out, going straight down at great speed. Too long in a straight-down dive and a wing could come off. Pull it out! Lacey eases the stick back, throttle already back. A tremendous weight sits on his shoulders and he is pushed down harder and harder into the seat. But the green below begins to move backwards and the nose is moving towards the horizon. The Hurricane is coming out. The blood drains from his head and then the force of gravity, the multiplied weight which has pressed him downward, begins to ease. He is levelling off though he has lost 5000 feet. The enemy and his comrades are out of sight.

He climbs to regain lost altitude, presses the microphone button just behind the throttle. 'Red Three to Red Leader. Where are you?' Over the receiver comes a reply: 'Red Leader to Red Three. Just north of Maidstone. Join up over Maidstone.' Lacey banks into a north-westerly heading to join up, eager to have company again. A lone fighter is easy prey. He gains steadily ... 12 000, 13 000, 14 000; twists his neck to check the sky behind him. No aircraft in sight. He can't be far from Pinetree squadron. The sky is empty and peaceful.

Then, ahead ... straight ahead, north-west ... specks ... growing rapidly larger. Fighter squadron. Lacey studies the fast approaching bogies ... single-engined aircraft ... perhaps 501. They come on. He can see the spinners. Yellow! Me.109s! Coming head-on. Have they seen him? He must act. He's on a collision course with a dozen enemy fighters, each faster than the Hurricane. Instinctively, he pushes the stick handle forwards, the horizon rises and he dives to pass beneath them. But he won't run away. By all the rules of aerial combat he should. He continues his dive, gaining speed, and now the 109s are directly above.

The rush of air and the roar of the engine increase as speed increases. Now he hauls back hard on the stick handle. He pulls the nose into the straight-up position. This time he has the speed to avoid a stall and the Hurricane rockets upwards. Lacey is now zooming skywards almost directly below the last 109 in the formation, keeping the stick back. The Hurricane, coming over on its back, levels out at the top of a loop directly behind the last enemy fighter. Lacey is upside down, held firmly by seat straps, eyes fixed on the Messerschmitt ahead. 150 yards! Perfect firing range. His loop was timed to perfection. He has never shot at another aircraft on his back. The gunsight is adjusted for a normal drop in the trajectory of shells from an upright position. He will have to allow for this and fire well above the 109! He must act, speed is falling. The 109s are cruising homeward at about 240 mph and though he has built up speed in his dive, when he loses that momentum the

109s can pull away. So far they haven't seen the audacious approach. He lines up the enemy wing-span in the glass.

Now. Fire! His thumb (pointing earthwards) pushes the button. Eight machine-guns spit a stream of armour-piercing and incendiary shells. Lacey, head down, watches the effect. The roar of his guns and the vibration of the aircraft add to the strange sensation of attacking on his back. But he has compensated accurately. The 109 staggers from the blast of close, concentrated fire. Incendiaries crash into the engine and into the fuel tank behind the pilot and in seconds a black stream of smoke pours out. Complete tactical surpise! Now the 109 turns out of formation, falls off to the side and bursts into flame. It plunges straight down.

Finally, Lacey rolls over. The blood drains from his head and he sees more clearly the eleven dark enemy fighters, crosses on their wings, directly ahead. Still they haven't seen him – or the destruction of their comrade to the rear! He manoeuvres in behind a 109 to the left . . . distance 250 yards, quickly he centres rudder and stick for proper altitude and lines him up in the sighting glass. Wing-span almost bar to bar, squarely in the orange circle. The firing button! For the third time the wing guns belch more than 100 shells a second. Though the pattern of fire is not fully concentrated at 250 yards, shells strike the second Me.109 instantly, tearing pieces out of fuselage and wings. Lacey holds the button down. More shells find the mark. The second victim now begins to stream white smoke. Lacey knows he's hit the coolant. The 109 is doomed, for without coolant the Daimler-Benz will overheat.

Lacey takes his finger off the firing button. The pilot will have to jump – over England or the Channel. Suddenly anti-aircraft fire begins to dot the sky. It bursts uncomfortably close. And at this moment the remaining ten enemy fighters, at last aware of an impudent intruder, do what they should have done in the beginning. They split into two groups, half turning right and half left. They are coming around to get behind him. If he turns after one group, the other will curve in behind. His ammunition is low. They have a speed advantage. He is certain to be caught from the rear by one half or the other! Yet he still has a few rounds and one 109 in the group banking left is trailing behind. Perhaps he just has time to get him and still get away. It's a gamble. Left rudder, left stick. Lacey leans into a hard left bank to line up behind him. The group to his right banks more sharply to come around behind. No doubt the enemy pilots can clearly see blue and red circles on the top of the turning Hurricane's wings and no doubt they admire the tenacity of this interceptor, who should be running away from the battle – who should not have initiated it at all.

Lacey keeps stick handle back, standing on his port wing, and lines up behind the last 109. He's at maximum range. Time is precious. Fire! For a second the Hurricane's eight guns lash out in a staccato. Then firing becomes erratic. One gun empties after the other. All silent. No more ammunition! He sees white streaks ahead, in front, on both sides. He's in the trap. The 109s which banked right are behind. Dive! Instinctively, his right hand pushes the stick handle forward and he almost lunges off the seat as the fighter's nose dips and dives for earth. Luckily, the Hurricane has a high initial rate of dive, faster than the Spit, and – Lacey hopes – fast enough to escape the 109s. He steals a march on the enemy, diving first. His momentum increases; unless they dive simultaneously, they cannot immediately catch him, and the 109s have limited fuel. Lacey is utilising the only advantage available under the circumstances – a good initial diving velocity. He spots a nearby cloud bank as he plummets downward. He'll slip into it and throw the 109s off if they're following him down.

Airspeed passes 300, 350, 400! Lacey plunges on, looking behind. He hurtles into the cloud bank ... down through the milky white and out again at the bottom. He eases back on the stick, constantly looking behind. The Hurricane's nose comes up. He's down to 3000 feet, still descending. He sees no one following! He reaches 1000, goes on down to the tops of the trees, and sets course for Kenley, north-west. Since the field is in the opposite direction to the Luftwaffe bases, perhaps their leader chose not to turn back, or couldn't because of fuel limitations. Thus Lacey finds himself free from pursuit but vulnerable at low altitude without ammunition and alone. He tensely scans the sky behind . . . no enemy aircraft. The lone fighter hurries along over the tree-tops.

For the first time since sighting the twelve enemy fighters Lacey begins to relax. Down below he recognises familiar landmarks; he's not far from Kenley. He will claim one victory, one probable, and damage to a third, having engaged four aircraft in all. And today he hasn't been hit, even though after the last attack it was close. (Lacey has crash-landed and parachuted so often lately he's relieved that today, with burned legs, he'll walk away from the landing.) Raising his nose and increasing altitude slightly every so often to get navigational bearings, he flies straight to Kenley. The green of the big field comes into view and is an inviting welcome; he circles preparatory to landing. Cleared to come in, he eases back on the throttle, drops flaps and, as speed lessens, lowers his undercarriage. The Hurricane glides downward at 120 mph. Just off the edge of the field he eases the nose upward and his speed comes back to 100.

The oil-spattered fighter touches down at 12.35 p.m. Pinetree Red Three is safely home. He slows the fighter and turns toward his revetment. His fitter and rigger are waiting, watching. Lacey, canopy open, brakes the Hurricane to a stop, pulls the throttle back. The engine continues to kick over and he reaches to two magneto switches at the bottom of the instrument panel and flips them off. The Rolls-Merlin dies. He pulls off his helmet, lifts himself out of the cockpit and begins to answer questions. He must tell the story – one enemy fighter surely shot down, one probable, with attacks on another and a bomber! Congratulations come from all sides of a gathering which has quickly assembled. The petrol lorry arrives and immediately begins to refuel the fighter.

Lacey walks to the dispersal hut where returning pilots

are gathered, discussing the flight. After a time the briefing officer asks casually: 'Anyone got anything to report?' Lacey is the only one who has. He hadn't mentioned it in the hut! He puts his combat report on paper and then is ready for lunch.

After eating, he comes back to the hut ... and finds himself again on readiness! He picks out a comfortable chair and tries to get some sleep, still thinking about shooting down an enemy fighter while on his back.

Later that afternoon the squadron was scrambled again. Once again Lacey was on the attack, intercepting a bomber force. Escorting 109s bounced the Hurricanes before they got into the bombers and in a dogfight with one Lacey shot the enemy's tail completely off with a concentrated pattern of fire. Shortly afterwards he caught one of the bombers (an He.111)[5] and sent it down – his second kill of the afternoon. In the course of one day he had destroyed an Me.109 in the morning and probably another and then added two victories in the afternoon! When he landed at Kenley he was tired but satisfied. Four victories in a day. This spirit, personified so well by Lacey, was what made it clear to the Luftwaffe across the Channel that the assault against England would not be as easy as it once looked.

By nightfall the Luftwaffe had flown 1300 sorties to carry out Goering's orders to destroy the remaining RAF fighters, which he claimed numbered only fifty. His pilots and bomber crews learned otherwise: as many as 370 RAF Hurricanes and Spitfires fought in each battle. German aircraft confirmed as destroyed numbered fifty-six, and an unknown number were too badly damaged to be immediately serviceable. The RAF lost twenty-six.

What Goering had boasted would be his day of triumph, with Britain left defenceless in the air and the coast open for the invading armies, had turned out a disaster. Two days later the German High Command issued a signal to the naval, army and air forces:

'Operation Sealion is postponed until further notice.'
The invasion barges and vessels were dispersed.

Daylight raids continued in decreased intensity.
Sergeant Lacey was again shot down on 17 September,
parachuting to land safely near Ashford, Kent. Ten days
later he shot down another Me. 109, and three more in
October. He was commissioned as an officer in January,
1941, flying with his squadron in sweeps over France.
He shot down three more Me. 109s during the summer
before being posted as an instructor. He returned to
combat duty in 1942 with 602 Squadron, and then in the
closing months of the war commanded 17 Squadron in
Burma. There he destroyed his twenty-eighth enemy aircraft, downing a Japanese Oscar II. After the war he
remained in the RAF until the age for retirement.

Notes

[1] All RAF squadrons had a call sign for communications. Pinetree was
that of 501. A squadron was divided into two flights; each flight into two
sections, given the name of colours. Each aircraft in a section had a
number.
[2] Orders and reports were transmitted in clearly understood words.
Vector meant turn (to the degrees of the compass stated). Angels meant
height with the number of thousands of feet. Bogies referred to enemy
aircraft. Tally-ho was the pilot's report of enemy sighted and going into
attack.
[3] The Me 109 could fly effectively about 2000 ft higher than a
Hurricane. Its maximum speed was 350 mph.
[4] The Dornier 17 was a twin-engine aircraft armed with two machine
guns and one cannon. Its maximum speed was 263 mph.
[5] The Heinkel 111 was a twin-engined aircraft armed with five machine
guns and one cannon. Its maximum speed was 245 mph.

BATTLE OF THE JAVA SEA

After the crippling blow inflicted on the US Pacific Fleet at Pearl Harbor on 7 December 1941, followed by the loss of the only British capital ships in the Far Eastern waters, *Prince of Wales* and *Repulse*, the Japanese navy and air force rapidly built up their forces in support of the spectacular advances of the armies. The aim was to capture the whole of the 'Southern Resources Area', vital both strategically and as a source of war materials. Aside from Malaya and the Philippines, already in Japanese hands, the richest zone was the British and Dutch East Indies. In the first few days of 1942 three Japanese amphibious groups, supported by aircraft carriers, secured bases in Borneo, Celebes, Bali, Java, and Sumatra. General Sir Archibald Wavell was put in command of the Allied units, made up of British, Australian, American and Dutch forces, in a valiant but vain effort to stem the advance of the enemy's overwhelming land, air and naval strength. On 25

February, the combined command of the Allied forces was abandoned, such men and material as still survived being transferred to Dutch direction. The following is an Australian war correspondent's account of the battle between the only surviving Allied ships in the area and a Japanese force commanded by Rear Admiral Takeo Takagi in the Java Sea.

HMAS *Perth* left Australia on her last voyage on 17 February 1942, when she drew out of Fremantle harbour and sailed northwards towards Java as escort to a small convoy of supply ships. Presently a radio signal ordered the ships to return to Fremantle, but a later signal told *Perth* to resume her original course alone. In all, *Perth* was recalled on three occasions, and then each time the decision was reversed. She finally reached Tanjong Pryok, the port of Batavia, on 24 February. On this and the following day Japanese planes raided the harbour, but their formation was broken up and the effectiveness of the raid was largely nullified by the barrage from *Perth*'s six-inch guns and smaller armament. The blasts from *Perth*'s big guns was such that hundreds of windows in the warehouses along the wharves were shattered. The one plane on *Perth* was ruined by blast from the four-inch guns of HMAS *Yarra*, moored alongside. Apart from damage to a small oil tanker, all the Japanese bombs missed their objectives. On 26 February *Perth* joined the other cruisers and destroyers in Sourabaya.

That evening, the Allied fleet under command of Admiral Doorman of the Dutch Navy, flying his flag on HNMS *De Ruyter*, sailed from Sourabaya to intercept a Japanese convoy reported to be approaching north-eastern Java. The Allied ships were two eight-inch gun cruisers, HMS *Exeter* and USS *Houston*, one six-inch gun cruiser, HMAS *Perth*, two 5·9-inch Dutch cruisers, HNMS *De Ruyter* and *Java*, as well as three British destroyers, *Electra*, *Encounter* and *Jupiter*, and four American and two Dutch destroyers.

HMAS *Perth* had already seen more action and sailed

farther on active service than any other cruiser in the Australian squadron. Commissioned in June 1939, she was diverted on her way home to Australia at the outbreak of the war to the West Indies Station, and spent the following months patrolling the central Atlantic and Caribbean Sea. *Perth* arrived in Sydney for the first time in March 1940, but after some months in Australian waters was sent to the Mediterranean. She was almost constantly in action in the ' eastern Mediterranean during the first half of 1941, and won distinction by her work off Greece and Crete and during the Syrian campaign. In August 1941 she was refitted and then carried out patrol duties in Australian waters until sent to Java in the third month of the Pacific war. *Perth*, of 6980 tons, carried eight six-inch and eight four-inch guns, apart from torpedo tubes and lighter armament. Her complement when she went into action in the Java Sea was about 680. She was commanded by Captain H. M. L. Waller, DSO and Bar, who had built up a magnificent record as commander of the Australian Destroyer Flotilla in the Mediterranean.

The fighting power of USS *Houston* had been already diminished, one of her gun turrets being out of action, thanks to enemy bombing in the Flores Sea. Japanese aircraft shadowed the Allied ships during the morning of 27 February, but no contact with enemy vessels was established until the middle of the afternoon, when Japanese cruisers and destroyers were sighted.

It has been estimated that the initial Japanese force in the battle of the Java Sea, which now commenced, comprised five cruisers and thirteen destroyers. But there are indications that at least one Japanese battleship and other cruisers took part in the later stages of the action. It is known that a number of Japanese submarines were operating in the area, but whether any of these was responsible for the torpedoing of Allied ships, or whether all torpedoes came from the destroyers is not certain.

Fire was opened by the heavy cruisers of both sides at 30 000 yards. The light cruisers and destroyers joined in as soon as they were within range. *Perth*'s second salvo hit a Japanese destroyer and the enemy flotilla retired into a smoke-screen. When the smoke cleared, the enemy destroyer was seen to be ablaze and there is little doubt that she sank.

Perth came under very heavy fire from one of the Japanese heavy cruisers, but neither then nor later in this action was she damaged in any way. Her next job was to effect a smoke-screen with destroyers around HMS *Exeter* which had been badly damaged in the engine-room by an enemy salvo. The Dutch destroyer *Witte de With*, screening *Exeter*, twice hit a Jap destroyer with her salvoes, but at this stage a torpedo struck the other Dutch destroyer amidships so that she broke in two and folded up like a jack-knife.

Admiral Doorman now made an attempt to get behind the enemy and attack his transports, and the Allied destroyers went into attack. As the light failed it appeared that HMS *Electra* battered an enemy destroyer with her gunfire, but she herself was then mortally hit. She stopped, and one by one her guns were silenced, until she sank just before dark.

The Japanese destroyers made another torpedo attack on *Perth* without success. One of the enemy vessels was hit and perhaps sunk during this attack. *Perth* then began a duel with an eight-inch cruiser and scored a series of hits. When the cruiser was last seen she was on fire and at a standstill with her stern well down.

Darkness now veiled the battle, in which contact between the ships had become very spasmodic. HMS *Jupiter* was torpedoed on the starboard side and put out of action. She sank before midnight.

The damaged *Exeter* with HMS *Encounter*, the four American destroyers and the surviving Dutch destroyer, managed to reach Sourabaya that night. The other four cruisers, having seen *Exeter* into safety, turned about again. Just before midnight *Perth* had another brush with the foe, scoring hits with at least two salvoes on an enemy cruiser.

Then disaster struck the Allied squadron.

The ships were proceeding in line ahead with the Admiral's flagship, *De Ruyter* leading, *Perth* next, then *Java*, with *Houston* bringing up the rear. Suddenly there was an explosion on *De Ruyter*, and *Perth* had to swerve to avoid the stricken ship which lost way and was soon aflame from stem to stern. A few minutes later there was a second explosion and *Java* dropped out of line.

Captain Waller, now left alone with *Houston* out of the fourteen ships which had opened the action in the afternoon, took violent evasive action immediately. It seems probable that the Dutch Admiral had run straight into a submarine trap and paid the penalty for having his ships in line-ahead formation. It is believed that a few score survivors from *De Ruyter* and *Java* subsequently reached the Java coast, but the majority of their crews were lost.

Of the ships which had returned to Sourabaya, only the four American destroyers escaped. *Witte De With* was bombed and sunk in Sourabaya harbour. *Exeter* and *Encounter*, which left on the night of 28 February, reported next morning that they had sighted a force of enemy ships. This was the last word received from them.

Perth and *Houston* reached Tanjong Pryok before noon on 28 February. Neither vessel could replenish the depleted stocks of ammunition for their bigger guns, but they did take on board some four-inch ammunition, oil fuel, additional fire-fighting equipment and a number of small rafts, which were to prove invaluable.

At Batavia Captain Waller conferred with Commodore J. A. Collins, formerly of HMAS *Sydney*, senior Australian naval officer in Java. It was decided that *Perth* and *Houston* should endeavour to pass through the confined waters of Sunda Strait during the night and then make for Tjilatjap, on the southern coast of Java. It was probably intended that they should evacuate Allied army and air force personnel who had been left on Java.

A report from Dutch headquarters which reached Captain Waller before the cruisers left Tanjong Pryok stated that aerial reconnaissance had failed to discover any signs of the enemy in Sunda Strait or its approaches. This report is one of the unexplained enigmas of the defence of Java. That evening *Perth* personnel plotted over 200 vessels – presumably all enemy – in the waters north of the island.

The superstitious had some grounds for feeling queasy before the Australian and American cruisers left port for the last time. In the first place, *Perth* had been recalled three times en route from Fremantle to Java. Secondly, there were two chaplains aboard – a bad omen. Both cruisers had taken on board a supply of rafts, a wise precaution but scarcely an encouraging one. The picture of Lord Nelson hanging in *Perth's* wardroom had dropped from the bulkhead in the Battle of the Java Sea and had not been restored to its place, but was left lying face downwards. Finally, the ship's mascot, a tabby cat named Red Lead, beloved by the crew, made repeated attempts to leave the ship before she sailed from Tanjong Pryok.

As the two cruisers drew out of the harbour, the horizon was clouded with billowing cumulus clouds, red in the sunset and shot through with lightning.

The last hour of February 1942 should find a permanent niche in the naval histories of Australia and the United States.

Just after eleven o'clock, three hours after leaving Batavia, one of the lookouts on *Perth*, which was leading, reported a dark object to starboard and, a few minutes later, the Australian cruiser opened fire from her forward turrets. *Perth* signalled that she had sighted a cruiser near Sunda Strait. This was the last word received about *Perth* or *Houston* until June, when a letter [by the author of this extract], read over Batavia radio by the Japanese, informed the people at home of the glorious final chapter in the history of the two cruisers.

Events now occurred with kaleidoscopic rapidity. It soon became apparent that a great number of enemy vessels lay around the two cruisers at the northern entrance to Sunda Strait. Almost immediately enemy salvoes were screaming over the Allied cruisers from many directions.

The gunners of *Perth* and *Houston* found targets looming up through the darkness at almost point-blank range. It appears that a huge enemy fleet, comprising aircraft-carriers, cruisers, destroyers, transports, tankers and supply ships, was about to launch the main Japanese landing on the north-west corner of Java in the region of Merak, at the entry to Sunda Strait. The transports and supply ships were drawn up in close formation in a huge crescent. *Perth* and *Houston* passed between ships and shore, belching shells from every gun that they could bring to bear. The enemy warships furiously replied.

At such range, even in the darkness, it was inevitable that both sides should wreak execution. However, thanks to Captain Waller's clever manoeuvring and the fact that he kept his ship down to half speed, nearly all the Japanese salvoes fell in front of the ships, causing no damage. But *Perth* and *Houston* had the kind of target which gunners dream about. As one of *Perth*'s torpedoemen said to me, 'You could see them now and then barely a mile away, dozens of 'em.'

One of *Houston*'s officers, who was on the bridge throughout the engagement, said, 'There was just a solid wall of enemy ships. You didn't have to sight. You just blazed away.' *Perth* used all her torpedoes, and it seems probable that most of them found their billets.

Despite the tornado of fire to which the Allied cruisers were exposed, it was twenty minutes before *Perth* was hit. The first shell to come aboard damaged the forward funnel, carried away a lifeboat, and wreaked havoc on the port pom-pom and flag-deck. Thereafter, both *Perth* and *Houston* were hit repeatedly, and about midnight two torpedoes struck *Perth*, the first on the starboard side, the second in the forward engine room. At the second hit the vessel began to lose way, and on the bridge Captain Waller exclaimed: 'That's torn it!'

Perth had now fired the last of her four-inch shells and had only a half-dozen six-inch left. The gunners kept blazing away with star shells and practice ammunition. *Houston* was also virtually out of ammunition. So close did Japanese destroyers come during the action that on several occasions the cruisers opened fire with their machine-guns. After the second torpedo hit *Perth*, Captain Waller gave the order, 'Abandon ship; every man for himself.' He was last seen standing on his bridge watching the last of the Carley floats thrown into the water.

As the vessel began to sink, she was hit by a third torpedo on the port side towards the stern. A fourth torpedo found its billet while some of the men were still clinging to her side as she began to slip more deeply into the water. She finally sank about 12.15 a.m. on 1 March. The tornado of enemy fire was now concentrated on *Houston*, and in the space of a few minutes she too was in a sinking condition. Less than twenty minutes after *Perth* had disappeared, *Houston* followed her to the bottom of Sunda Strait.

Grievous as the loss of Allied men and ships was, the infinitely superior Japanese naval force gained a costly victory. Three cruisers, nine destroyers, a converted aircraft-carrier and three troop transports were either sunk or had to be beached. On *Houston* and *Perth* many of the crews were trapped below deck and went down with their ships. As many who got into the water were either suffocated by fuel oil slicks or wounded by the shells and torpedoes aimed to finish off the sinking vessels. A few survivors managed to get ashore in Borneo and Java. Some 200 were lifted from rafts and floats by the Japanese. In all 350 of *Houston*'s crew and 330 from *Perth* survived the battle, most to be taken prisoner; some to die later in prison camps. Ten days after the battle the Dutch East Indies capitulated, and the invaders achieved a foothold in New Guinea and the Solomon Islands. But the tide of war was beginning to turn. The US Admiral Chester Nimitz was appointed Naval C-in-C, Pacific, and the inexorable progress to the defeat of Japan had begun.

THE NIGHT OF 23 OCTOBER 1942

From the autumn of 1940 fighting in the desert of North Africa had been almost continuous, at first with the Italians, and after February 1941 with General Erwin Rommel's armoured force, soon to be known as the Afrika Corps. Thereafter the war fluctuated between victories and defeats on both sides, until by the summer of 1942 the enemy seemed poised for the invasion of Egypt, endangering Britain's oil supplies from the Middle East and cutting the sea, air and land routes to the Far East and Australasia.

The British Commonwealth forces were manning the last defensive position west of the Nile Delta – a strip of land between the sea and a salt marsh called El Alamein. Here, both sides knew, the fate of the Middle East and perhaps the outcome of the war itself would be decided.

On 13 August 1942 Lieutenant-General Bernard Montgomery took over command of the 8th Army. Rommel, knowing that the new commander was building up massive forces, hurriedly prepared to attack. He did so at Alma Halfa, to the south of El Alamein. He failed to break through and after six days of bitter fighting withdrew. By then he was a sick man and returned to Germany for medical treatment.

Montgomery immediately began to draft his plan for a decisive battle. He had six weeks for his programme of retraining, reorganisation and rehearsal, plus the planning for deploying the vast intake of men, tanks, guns, ammunition, fuel and food for what was to be one of the most meticulously planned battles in British military history.

D-Day approached. The waiting tanks and guns prepared to move into their secret positions. Maintained at an even flow, the transport companies continued daily to augment the mounting piles of shells, cartridges, bombs, hand grenades and all the other stores of war. The artificers and mechanics tested and serviced the guns, tanks, aircraft, armoured cars and small arms under their care. As it was before Agincourt,

> The armourers, accomplishing the knights,
> With busy hammers closing rivets up,
> Give dreadful note of preparation.

Staff officers worked far into the night at plans, maps, air photographs, intelligence reports, administrative instructions, operation orders and march tables.

Yet none but a few knew what lay ahead. In the forward localities the infantry and the artillery observation officers gazed out over the sere and shadowless wastes ahead, seemingly devoid of life but dotted with the shapes of burnt-out tanks, of wrecked vehicles and of scattered remnants of equipment, 'where black death keeps record of his trophies'. Nightly, the infantry patrols continued silently to range the wide expanses of No Man's Land, seeking information of the enemy. Daily the squadrons of the air, 'with strong wings scaling the upward sky', bent their bright courses. The nights grew colder; men wore their battledress blouses in the evening and the early morning, and their greatcoats by night. But the middle hours of the day were very hot still.

The first blows were struck from the air. They were aimed at securing superiority over the enemy air forces from D-Day onwards, so that there would be the minimum interference with our ground operations and so that the Desert Air Force and their cooperating squadrons from that day onwards could concentrate on attacking the enemy's forward troops.

Coningham[1] began, accordingly, with heavy bombing attacks on the enemy airfields. On 19 October the German fighter airfields at El Daba were attacked by Baltimores of 55th and 223rd Squadrons, fighter-bombers of 2nd and 4th Squadrons South African Air Force and by the Royal Australian Air Force. Night attacks followed by Bostons, their targets illuminated by Albacores of the Fleet Air Arm.

Next day the Italian airfields at Fuka were bombed and another punishing visit paid to El Daba. On the 21st the Wellingtons joined in. Blow followed blow. By day and by night the attacks were kept up until the 23rd without intermission. By the 23rd, at a cost of only thirteen British aircraft and one American, our fighter patrols roamed over the enemy's forward airfields continuously without challenge, complete masters of the air. In readiness for the next phase of close engagement and pursuit, Coningham moved two fighter wings forward to advanced airfields at El Hammam.

The time drew near for all men to be taken into the Army Commander's trust.

On 19 and 20 October Montgomery made his memorable expositions at the Amariya Cinema to all officers down to the rank of lieutenant-colonel of how the battle was to be fought, how it would develop and how long it would last. It was an occasion not likely to be forgotten by those who attended. To many it was a day of revelation.

Montgomery explained his plan in detail. He estimated the battle would last for twelve days. Veterans of the desert war had accepted the appointment of a new Commander with some cynical scepticism. But they left that cinema utterly convinced that unequivocal victory was at last to be their reward.

On 21 October, on Montgomery's orders, the COs themselves broke the news to all their own junior officers and men, sitting silent and absorbed in semicircles on the sand, with diagrams of the coming battle before them and with the sun blazing down on their bronzed limbs. From that briefing no man was excluded except only those who were then in the foremost positions, lest they should be raided by the enemy, and those who were to go out on patrol.

On that day all leave was quietly stopped without any official announcement. Thenceforward 8th Army was safely locked up without bars in the great immensity of the desert. On the same day Montgomery paid a final visit to the assaulting divisions to see if they were all 'well and comfortable'. He found the Army's morale, he declared, 'on the top line'.

Few men who were in the desert at that hour will ever lose the memory of the heartening breath that swept across the sandy wastes and rocky desolations, that blew invigoration into the cramped trenches, the sweating gun pits, the close-battened tanks and the expectant squadrons of the air. It was tremendously exciting, tremendously challenging. An Army whose pride and spirit was always high became infused with a new buoyancy of spirit and a new conviction of their power to win. Lieutenant-Colonel Bob Turner, addressing his Second-13th Australian Battalion and feeling the inspiration of Montgomery's address, gave them his own text from *Macbeth* to take into battle: 'Be bloody, bold and resolute'.

Major Jack Perrott, addressing his sappers of 2nd Cheshire Field Squadron and striving to pass on to them the enthusiasm he had caught when Gatehouse addressed the officers of 10th Armoured Division, declared that 'the battle was won before it had started'. Sapper Flinn, of the companion 3rd Cheshire Field Squadron, felt an exhilaration never experienced on the eve of any other battle. 'The dynamic little man in the funny hat', he said, 'convinced us entirely that we were going to win and that the shambles of the past were over.'

Harding, the new commander of 7th Armoured Division, recorded that 'the atmosphere of well-designed, objective preparations, lively expectancy and quiet confidence pervaded the division and indeed the whole Army'. McCreery, Alexander's Chief of Staff, severe, matter-of-fact and emphatically no 'Monty man', declared that the morale of the infantry was 'sky-high'. Briggs observed that there was 'a lighter spring in men's steps', a confidence in their bearing, a new ring in their voices, and a positive direction in their thinking.

Kippenberger, breaking the news to 23rd New Zealand Battalion, whom he had selected for the first violent burst into the enemy lines, told them that this was the greatest moment of their lives. Theirs was the duty and the honour of breaking in. 'I expect you to do it', he said, 'whatever the cost.'

Romans, the battalion's ardent CO, a man who in battle burned with fires of exaltation, called the men to their feet and led them in 'three fierce, and thundering cheers.'[2]

The evening sandstorms blew up, the empty petrol tins bowled along before the wind, banging like fire-crackers, the flies swarmed under a torrid sun, the screaming Stukas dive-bombed occasionally from the brazen sky, the shells and machine-guns crackled, as of old, but a new stimulus and a new purposefulness were clearly abroad in that far desert.

Extraordinary measures were taken, under the *Bertram* plan, to conceal from the enemy the last moves forward. On the night of 20 October, 1st and 10th Armoured Divisions began to move up by stages to their assembly areas behind 30th Corps front. The main bodies immediately sank into wireless silence, but small detachments selected from men with 'recognisable voices', whom the enemy would already have heard talking on the air, were left behind in the training areas to maintain a simulation of normal wireless activity. Gatehouse himself, together with Bill Liardet, his GSO 1, had to journey back so that their well-known voices could be heard.

On reaching the assembly areas, tanks, guns and vehicles slipped secretly into the positions occupied by the dummies of the *Bertram* plan. From then on no movement of men or vehicles was allowed by day except what was unavoidable. No smoke from fires, no lights, no washing, no airing of beds, no digging. Tracks made by the tanks moving in were obliterated by dragging wire trailers along them.

The utmost care was demanded to ensure that, on the featureless ground and in the dark, the assaulting infantry of 30th Corps should start on the right line in relation to the artillery barrage and keep its ordered direction. On 51st Division's front, Lieutenant-Colonel J. C. Stirling, of the 5th Seaforth Highlanders, virtually lived for four days and nights in No Man's Land, identifying and marking exactly the 2500 yards of start-line, and clearing and marking the nine lanes leading up to it through our own minefields. The start-line was to be a few hundred yards out in No Man's Land. To find the exact pin-points of each terminal, he employed officers converging from various directions, marching by compass and counting their paces. These lines were required to be marked with nine miles of white tape, but, in order that they should not be observed from the air or by an enemy patrol, he laid them out first with telephone wire, ready to be quickly replaced by tape on the night of the 23rd itself.

On the night of 22 October the assaulting infantry of 30th Corps, the heavily-laden machine gunners, the artillery Forward Observation Officers and the engineers of the mine-clearing teams, lit by an early moon, moved quietly forward to the shallow slit trenches that had previously been dug, camouflaged and provisioned, on the home edge of our own minefield, steel-helmeted, equipped and ready for the great test.

The next morning, which was a Friday, Montgomery himself moved forward to a small tactical headquarters, alongside those of Leese, Lumsden and Coningham, their vehicles all dug-in.

All that day the waiting soldiers in front remained motionless in their cramped trenches, forbidden to move for any purpose whatever, roasted and blistered by a blazing sun and preyed upon by clouds of flies. They spoke a little to one another and tried to get some sleep, but for the most part each man was occupied with his private thoughts. It was an extremely trying day, the physical discomfort aggravated by the high tension of expectancy. Peter Moore and his minefield sappers of 10th Armoured Division felt 'all very keyed up and a bit frightened, but determined that the thing was going to work this time, for we had so often seen it go wrong before'.

The long, burning day dragged on. The waiting soldiers felt as though cut off from the world. Before them stretched a country seemingly as empty and barren as it had been for thousands of years, shadowless and motionless, except for the 'Devil's Waters', the dancing mirages of the afternoon, but, as well they knew, impregnated with the buried engines of death and peopled with the unseen outposts of the distant enemy. As the day wore on, every man began that small and meaningful gesture which he was to repeat with increasing frequency in every hour to come – looking at his watch.

The sun began to sink in a crimson bed behind the enemy lines. The charged air gave up its burden of heat and the cool evening breeze mercifully flowed in, expelling the hateful flies. A meditative colonel closed his sketch-book with a sigh and put away his pencil. The twilight phantasms dissolved. Suddenly it was dark. The myriad stars began their nightly watch. The chill of evening made men shiver a little.

The soldiers got up from their cramped trenches, their

accoutrements creaking as they stretched, moved about and relieved themselves. Hot meals came up from the battalion lines in the rear. Officers and NCOs went up and down, checking equipment and ammunition and ensuring the utmost quiet. Water-bottles were inspected. A tin of bully beef and a packet of ration biscuits were issued to each man.

Out in front of 51st Division, Stirling and his men of 5th Seaforth Highlanders, spectral shadows working against time, quickly ran out the white tapes of the start-line in No Man's Land and lit the pinpoint lamps that showed each battalion its way ahead through our own minefield. At the Regimental Aid Posts, the Medical Officers, among the very bravest of all men on the battlefield, with their orderlies and their stoical stretcher-bearers, prepared to be about their business, and there, also, were likely to be found the battalion padres.

The main tracks from the rear built by 30th Corps on the northern front – Sun, Moon, Star, Bottle, Boat and Hat – were likewise lit with their distinguishing signs. The anti-tank guns, bren-carriers and other operational vehicles of the infantry moved up and parked, to await their chance to traverse the minefields. The divisional commanders and brigadiers drove forward to their tactical battle head-quarters in the vicinity of the front line. The Valentines of 23rd Armoured Brigade, having, like chrysalids, cast off the canvas skins of their dummies, emerged in their fighting aspect and crawled forward to mate with the infantry whom they were to accompany – Finigan's and Clarke's to the Australians, Cairns's to the Highlanders, Winberg's to the South Africans. John Currie, bubbling with laughter at the prospect of action, brought up his more powerful tanks to the New Zealand sector, the formidable shapes of the new Shermans silhouetted against the background of the stars; it was the first time that the American tank had been summoned into battle and in the mustering squadrons all ranks braced themselves for the challenge to its baptism of fire. Pat Hobart, Currie's brigade major, wrote in his diary: 'My mind stopped revolving over and over, checking over every detail of plans, orders and preparations. If anything had been forgotten, it was too late now to do anything about it. Felt rather tense but somehow fatalistic.'

Montgomery's battle message was read out to the troops, in which he declared his confidence that if every officer and man entered upon this battle with the determination to fight and kill and win, 'we will hit the enemy for "six" right out of North Africa'. Then he went on:

> Let every officer and man enter the battle with a stout heart, and with the determination to do his duty so long as he has breath in his body.
>
> And let no man surrender so long as he is unwounded and can fight.
>
> Let us all pray that 'the Lord Mighty in battle' will give us the victory.

Men looked again at their watches.

The infantry started to fall in by platoons and to move forward throughout our own minefield to the white tapes of the start-line in No Man's Land. In the New Zealand Division Reg Romans, eager and ardent, his shirt sleeves rolled up, led his battalion forward with sections in single file, fifty yards apart. To Lieutenant John Van Grutten and Sapper Flinn, both of 3rd Cheshire Field Squadron, the scene looked for all the world like the start of some great and stern athletics contest.

In 51st Division every man was wearing a white St Andrew's cross on his back as a recognition signal in the dark and in 1st Gordon Highlanders every officer was carrying a rifle like his men. The machine gunners of the Middlesex Regiment, one platoon to each battalion of Highland infantry, took up their heavy loads – seven men to a gun, carrying gun, tripod, water and ammunition for their 6000 yards carry. Wimberley, the knees of his long legs drawn up to his chin, drove up in his jeep to his battle head-quarters in the front line. He looked at the gaps in our own minefield and saw that they were properly lit for the move forward to the start-line.

'As we drove about', he records in his journal, 'everything was deathly silent. I remembered First Cambrai, in 1917, how quiet it was before Zero. It seemed a good omen. Then I stood at one of the minefield gaps and watched my Jocks filing silently through, heavily laden with picks, shovels and sandbags, as well as their weapons and accoutrements. At the head of each battalion was its CO, his piper at his side. It was only possible now for me to pray. I went back to my battle headquarters and had a little food.' The generals had now handed over to the regimental soldiers.

At the start-line the infantry, the minefield sappers and the machine gunners spread out in their correct order in the spacing at which they were to advance. At a quiet order the infantry fixed bayonets. The navigating officers, compass in hand, took station in the centre of each battalion and company. The taping squads fell in immediately behind them, ready to reel out the white line of the battalion axis.

Dead silence lay over the whole desert. The swelling moon rode high, large, serene, illuminating the spectral scene with blue light. By its bright light men peered again at their watches, waiting for the mighty roar which they knew would burst out behind them at twenty minutes to ten.

Every man in 8th Army and the Desert Air Force now had his eye on his watch, counting the minutes. Behind the infantry, where the hidden armoured divisions lay, the flimsy structures of the dummy lorries were cast aside, to reveal to the inscrutable moon the naked features of guns and tanks. On the Springbok Road, just south of El Alamein Station, 1st and 10th Armoured Divisions, after a difficult and skilfully planned approach march, refreshed and took such rest as they could until their turn to go forward at 2 a.m. In the Warwickshire Yeomanry a radio set picked up the air of 'The White Cliffs of Dover' on the BBC.

Robert Wright, commanding 76th Anti-tank Regiment in 1st Armoured Division, wrote in his journal: 'I could not help having a feeling of pride and confidence; proud to be taking part in a battle likely to prove decisive, confident that the leadership, the men, the tanks, the guns and the aircraft were now enough to deliver a real punch. Except for one or two vehicles moving on the coast road, everything was very still. The scene reminded me of the marshalling of the performers before entry into the arena at the Aldershot Tattoo. Even now our eyes were focused on Tripoli, 1300 miles away!'

On the airfields away in the rear the bomb racks had been charged and the air crews briefed for the night's tasks. They were to illuminate the enemy country by flares, bomb gun positions, attack concentrations of troops with low-flying aircraft, jam the enemy's radio by specially-equipped Wellingtons, lay clouds of smoke to create confusion and drop dummy parachutists.

The Royal Navy also had their part to play and a small force had put out to sea. Their task, with RAF co-operation, was to make a feint landing in the enemy's rear at Ras el Kenayis, a promontory near Fuka, with the intention of creating confusion and nervousness and of occupying the enemy's reserves.

That evening Stumme radioed his routine evening report to Hitler's headquarters in Germany: *Enemy situation unchanged.*

Meanwhile, a little way behind the infantry were the men who were counting first the minutes and then the seconds perhaps more precisely than anyone else – the artillery.

At the appointed second, 882 field and medium guns were to open fire, in Montgomery's words to the author, 'like one battery'. For this second the gunners had been preparing all day and the gunnery staffs for much longer. The fire plan prepared by Kirkman for the whole thirty-eight miles from the sea to Himeimat had been allotted and sub-allotted from Army to Corps, Corps to division, division to regiment and regiment to battery. The gunners' maps were covered with transparent traces on which were marked with precise care the parallel lines by which a curtain of shells would move forward by leaps of 100 yards for the whole depth of the infantry's advance.

But it was not to be a 'barrage' in the true sense; there were not enough guns for that. On the New Zealand front, as an example, there would be only one shell every forty-five yards. It was to be mainly a series of moving concentrations of shell fire on known or suspected points of enemy resistance. The first fifteen minutes, however, were to be devoted to concentrations on the enemy's own gun positions, plotted from air photographs and by other means, in order to reduce the volume of fire that would break on our infantry.

At the little headquarters of each battery – usually a hole dug out of the sand and rock – the Command Post Officer and his assistants, working with artillery board, range table and slide rule, had patiently calculated the line and range for each of the eight guns of their battery for every step in the long ladder of fire. The arithmetical corrections had been applied for the barometric pressure, the temperatures of the air and the cartridge, the direction and force of the wind, the difference in height above sea level between each gun and its target. Still further corrections had to be made for each gun individually, as also for each batch of shells and cartridges if they differed from the normal.

The Command Post of each battery was quite close to the two Troops of four guns and before long the completed gun programmes, which were foolscap forms covered with a mass of figures, went out to the Gun Position Officer of each Troop, who was a subaltern. The GPO, through his Tannoy loudspeaker set, or by other means, then summoned his four Nos. 1, who commanded each gun and who were nearly all sergeants, and explained his task to each. There was a start of astonishment when he told them that they would have to fire 600 rounds per gun that night.

Back in each gun pit, under its dun camouflage net, the No. 1 went through the barrage programme with his gun-layer, explained the task to his detachment and prepared his ammunition, which for days had been gradually accumulating and had lain buried in the sand. He saw that water was at hand for sponging out the gun when it became over-hot, ensured that all moving parts were working smoothly and tested his sights. An artificer came round to test the gun's recoil apparatus.

Every man in the detachment now knew the nature of the tremendous call that was to be made on him. It was to be the most massive artillery onslaught ever seen in the continent of Africa and the biggest of the British Army anywhere since 1918. Except for ten minutes' rest each hour to cool the gun, they would be required to maintain a high rate of fire for five and a half hours continuously, and if they came under fire themselves from the enemy must not pause or take cover. When all was prepared, the sweating detachment bedded down in the sand for what rest they could get.

The quick desert twilight fell and all down the long line 8th Army awoke to sudden activity. The gunners saw a flood of traffic crawling forward – tanks, scout cars, carriers, lorries – and great clouds of dust were kicked up, neutralising the moonlight. In the rear of the gun position, the pin-point lamp had been lit on the night picket, on which the layer would centre the vertical cross wires of his dial sight to put his gun on the right line.

The men had a hot evening meal and looked at their watches, as everyone throughout the Army was doing. Through the camouflage net overhead the moon glinted wanly on the polished parts of the gun. The GPO went quietly round the Troop to see that all was well. The men began to break open the green metal ammunition boxes. Though the night air was chill, they stripped to the waist, for soon they would be dripping with sweat.

At about 9.30 the GPO, from his position in the centre rear of the Troop, ordered crisply: 'Take post!'

The faint moon-shadows were agitated into sudden life as the gun detachment sprang to their places — No. 2 on the right ready to operate the breech mechanism, the layer on the left at his dial sight, with the elevating and traversing wheels at his hand, the other numbers at the trail or by the stacked ammunition. The No. 1 ordered: 'HE, 117, Charge 3, load.'

The layer set his driftscale plate and range reader to the Charge 3 settings, No. 4 stepped forward with the 25-lb high-explosive shell, armed with its instantaneous 117 fuse, and slipped it into the open breech of the gun. No. 1 himself, with a short, truncheon-like rammer, rammed the shell home and as the copper driving-band engaged with the rifling of the barrel there was a deep, bell-like ring. No. 4 half-turned, took the long, brass cartridge case from No. 5, showed it to No. 1 to prove that it contained the full three charges of propellant, and pushed it into the breech with his closed fist. No. 2 slammed home the breech-block with a metallic clang.

The sergeant ordered: 'Zero one five degrees.'

By the light of a hand torch the layer set the scale on his dial sight to the figure which would bring his gun pointing towards its target and, by means of hand signals, directed the trail to be swung over until he found the light on the night-aiming-point in the prisms of his sight.

'Angle of sight 5 minutes elevation.'

The enemy battery was a little higher above sea level than his gun and the layer made the correct setting on his sight clinometer.

'10 800.'

The layer, repeating '10 800', quickly set the range to the enemy battery on his range-scale plate. The muzzle of the gun lifted up and up as he turned the elevating handwheel for approximate elevation first. He cross-levelled his sight till it was vertical, then, with his eye glued to the rubber eyepiece, laid accurately on the night aiming-point and finally levelled his sight clinometer bubble for exact elevation. Then he reported: 'Ready.'

The gun was ready to be fired, the detachment alert and tensed, but there were still some minutes to go. The GPO ordered: 'Troop, rest.'

The detachment relaxed, but stayed at their posts. Someone cracked a little joke and there was a subdued laugh. The sergeant was looking at his watch continuously and presently he said: 'A minute to go'. The last long seconds dragged by till at last there was a crisp command, from the GPO: 'Take post!'

Alert and keyed once more, like runners poised for the starting pistol, the detachment, at their action positions, awaited the ultimate order. There was a tingling silence over all the desert as the moon and the multitudinous stars looked down on an army waiting to spring.

At forty seconds before zero, when the first shell was due to burst on its target, came at last the order: 'B Troop, fire!'

The Battle of El Alamein had begun.

The storm of the Alamein barrage ripped through the sky on a front of thirty-eight miles. High above the screaming shells forty-eight Wellingtons dropped 125 tons of bombs on enemy gun positions. Then the masses of infantry marched forward to the attack behind the armour.

For eight days and nights the battle continued unabated, culminating in Montgomery's final knockout: Operation Supercharge. Rommel, back from sick leave, ignored Hitler's command to stand fast, and saved the remnants of his forces from utter annihilation by ordering a general withdrawal, with the British relentlessly pursuing them as far as Sollum. Next day Anglo-American troops under General Eisenhower landed at Oran, Casablanca, and near Algiers.

The pride of the Nazi armies, the Afrika Corps, was shattered, its divisions merely token numbers. Three Italian divisions had virtually ceased to exist.

In celebration of one of the most historic victories in the annals of war the church bells of Britain rang out for the first time in three years.

Notes

[1] Air Vice-Marshal Arthur Coningham, in command of Western Desert Air Force.

[2] Major-General Sir Howard Kippenberger, in his book 'Infantry Brigadier'. He commanded the 5th New Zealand Infantry Brigade.

ODETTE, GC

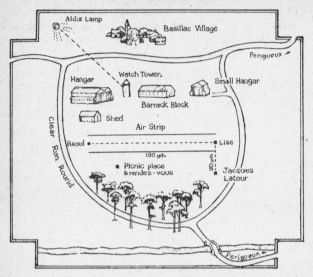

Odette Marie Céline Sansom, born in France, married to an Englishman, and the mother of three young daughters, was thirty years old when she volunteered to join the French Section of Special Operations Executive, formed soon after Germany conquered France in 1940. SOE's purpose was to support resistance to the Nazis in occupied Europe, and to recruit British agents to fight and work beside the patriots.

After rigorous training Odette, Number S.23 in the SOE files and Madame Odette Metayer, widow of an employee in a Boulogne shipping agency, according to her forged identity papers and ration card, sailed in October 1942, on a troopship to Gibraltar. She was then taken by a sardine fishing smack to a deserted spot on the rocky coast of France near Cassis, 23 kilometres east of Marseille. To the men of the French freedom fighters who met her on the night of 1-2 November she was known simply by the cover name of Lise.

Her orders were to report to Raoul, the key British agent in the South of France. Raoul was the cover name of Captain Peter Churchill. His duties were to organise arrivals of agents by submarine, fishing boat, parachute or RAF Lysander, getting them out of the country when danger became too great; to maintain coded wireless contact with London; and to arrange for drops of arms, explosives, food and money. Raoul also had to weld the separate groups of resistance fighters into a unified force. This was a formidable task. Gaullists were wary of Leftist guerilas. All were fiercely patriotic and resented any idea that Britain should control their every action.

Odette, as Lise, duly contacted Raoul at his hide-out in Cannes and became his courier and principal assistant. She began work at a time when rivalry between the various groups had reached a state of near-chaos, occasionally with actual fighting over arms and supplies dropped by the RAF. Their impatience to be in the vanguard of the struggle against the Nazis brought needless danger from the real enemies – the Gestapo and German army counter-intelligence, the Vichy police, and traitors ready to sell their compatriots for reward. Raoul realised that he would have to report in person to London so that SOE could devise proper control of these brave but undisciplined freedom fighters. London agreed that he should return. RAF Intelligence named a small disused airfield at Basillac, a village near Perigueux in the Dordogne, for a Lysander to touch down briefly for the pick-up. Time, date, and place were subject to Raoul checking that the airfield was still suitable and reasonably safe. As soon as Raoul reported that all was well, SOE would confirm that the plan would go ahead with a BBC message 'Les femmes sont parfois volages' ('Women are sometimes fickle'). There was a certain wry humour about the sentence, for London also agreed with Raoul that Lise was certainly not fickle and could take over her chief's duties while he was absent. Raoul made preparations for a detailed reconnaissance of the airfield.

Methodically, Raoul began to plan the operation. Paul Frager,[1] his fellow-passenger, was at the moment in Lyon so a courier was sent to that city to summon him to a rendezvous at Perigueux which Raoul decided should be operational HQ. Not only was Perigueux the obvious place but its *foie gras* was famous throughout France. It would be pleasant to bring home a jar for Buck[2] who had a cultured palate. . . . The next thing was to inform Marsac,[3] then in Marseille, of the plan and to ask him for the loan of a receiving-set to pick up the BBC message on the spot, so another courier was dispatched hot-foot to Marseille. In case the field proved on inspection to be useless, Arnaud[4] was consulted and two alternative innocent-sounding code messages were devised by which London would know whether to carry on or to call the whole thing off. He – Arnaud – would transmit the chosen message immediately he received a telephone call from Lise from Perigueux. That disposed of Cannes. Raoul packed cheerfully and set out with Odette by train for Perigueux – a distance of some 320 miles.

At Marseille, the always reliable Marsac was waiting on the platform. Through the window of Raoul's second-class compartment, he passed a receiving set to Odette – who graciously accepted the assistance of a German officer in placing it on the luggage rack. It was, she said, very kind of him and he said that it was a pleasure. 'Your suitcase, madame, is heavy enough to be a radio set,' he said with a guffaw and Odette smiled a little wanly. At Toulouse, Raoul and she changed trains and travelled uncomfortably through the night arriving at Perigueux in time for lunch.

Neither of them had ever been in Perigueux before nor had they any contact there. It was always unwise to indicate that one was a stranger by asking questions and it was thus with a completely false air of assurance that they entered the town. In the main square stood the Grand Hotel and, to their surprise and gratification, rooms happened to be available – albeit in the attic. As it would be necessary to listen in to the BBC in the hotel, the humble position of their rooms suited them admirably. The fact that the dining room was cluttered up with German officers was compensated for by the excellence of lunch, and Raoul wavered a little in his decision to present Buckmaster with a jar of *pâtè-de-foie-gras*. His aim was to eat all he could get himself. A glass of *Marc* merely confirmed this gluttonous wish.

Immediately after lunch, he and Odette hired two *vèlo-taxis* and told the muscular cyclists that they wanted to go to Basillac. Though she disliked *vèlo-taxis* on principle because a human being took the place of a horse, she sat with composure in the trailer while the sweating young man pedalled up the hills. She had time to reconsider her view. There was, after all, about a *vèlo-taxi* a refreshing absence of noise – if one could ignore the gasps and grunts of the rider. Surely the majority of the world's ills sprang from the invention of the internal combustion engine. While musing idly on this sad and well-worn theme, she had noticed and marked down for future reference the exact position of an aerodrome on the left – the philosophical and the practical being nicely mixed in her blood. Arrived at Basillac, she and Raoul paid the exorbitant sum demanded by their *conducteurs* and dismissed them. They had, they said, decided to take the bus back after a walk to settle their over-taxed digestions.

They had not only noticed the airfield. They had also remarked on the disturbing presence of a hangar, a building that looked remarkably like a barrack-block and a control tower. The great question was still to be solved. Were these ominous buildings occupied or not?

Arm in arm, Raoul and Odette sauntered round the field. To the casual observer, they were merely a flirtatious couple taking the air. In intervals between calculating the field's layout and the distance from the road to the hangar, Raoul gave her an occasional bucolic nudge and Odette produced in reply the traditional rustic giggle. The buildings were definitely if sparsely occupied. On the other hand, flowing behind a clump of trees, there was river with a bridge on the far side of the airfield and this bridge would make an excellent escape route after the operation, leading, as it did, to dense woods. Weighing up the merits and drawbacks of the field – and not forgetting the 300 miles they had travelled to get here – Raoul and Odette decided that the operation stood rather more than a fair chance of success. They walked the ten kilometres back to Perigueux and, after dinner, Odette put through a guarded trunk call to Arnaud in Cannes. The operation was on.

Next morning, a new difficulty arose. Somehow a plug had to be found to fit the wire of the receiving set into the electric light socket. This essential part – like every other radio part – was illegal to sell, and any attempt to purchase it might lead to arrest. Without it, it would be impossible to listen in to the BBC. Odette used her lipstick to best advantage, put on her smartest hat and her air of damsel-in-distress and sallied forth into the town. She was back within half an hour with the plug in her handbag. When they met Paul Frager and his lieutenant Jacques Latour[5] punctually to the minute in a café, it seemed that fate at last must be with them.

It was agreed that Paul and Jacques should dine together on the terrace of the hotel while Raoul listened in upstairs to the BBC. As he plugged in to the electric light switch, it occurred to him that the walls were remarkably thin and it was little comfort to remember that only that morning, the Vichy police had arrived and arrested the man who had slept last night in the next room. He found considerable difficulty in getting the BBC at all on the new, unfamiliar set and, when he did get what he thought must be their wavelength, a fearful caterwauling and wailing sounded all over the attic. He switched it off and wiped his forehead. He must try again because, in three minutes, the transmission would be over. Hopelessly, he moved the needle to another station. The first words he heard came through, clear as a cow-bell.

'*Les femmes sont parfois volages. . . .*'

It took Raoul about three minutes to pack. He strolled leisurely downstairs, cancelled dinner and his room and explained that he had met some old friends who had asked him to stay with them. While Odette paid her bill and told some equally plausible story, Raoul sauntered out to the Terrace where Paul and Jacques were studying the menu and wondering what to have after their *pâté-de-foie-gras*. His news decided them and all they asked for was the bill. By a quarter past eight, all four conspirators were marching gladly along the road to Basillac at a steady four miles an hour, their heads high and their eyes on the moon that was rising like a gigantic blood-orange behind the jet-black fretwork of the trees.

At ten to ten they reached the road leading to the airfield. Over the grass a white mist lay waist-deep under the moon and the night was very cold and still.

A whispered conference was held at the field's corner and, by the shaded light of a torch, Raoul indicated the general layout and where he had decided to place the flare-path. The first thing to do was to circumnavigate the field so that Paul and Jacques should get the feel of the ground. Then, having marked down the angles of the L-shaped flare-path, they should all four rendezvous at the fringe of the copse and wait. As soon as the Lysander appeared, Raoul and Paul should run to the top of the 'L' 's upright, Lise should station herself at its right angle and Jacques at the end of the horizontal. Once the aircraft had touched down, Raoul and Paul would scramble in and take off while Lise and Jacques would meet again by the copse and together make their way across the river bridge and through the woods, rejoining the main road to Perigueux lower down. Speed was the absolute essential, for the moment they heard the aircraft coming in to land the guards would be out. With any luck, the Lysander's wheels would not have to rest on French soil longer than ninety seconds and Raoul sincerely hoped it wouldn't come in until after midnight when some, at least, of the guards might be expected to be in bed and, as it were, temporarily, *hors de combat*.

By twenty-past ten the flare-path had been marked out and white handkerchiefs left on the ground to indicate each person's position. The mist was rising and soon the airfield would be as light as day. Odette opened her rucksack and produced her invariably first-class supper of smoked ham, Camembert and Armagnac. Sitting shivering in the shadow of the trees, she asked Raoul to give her messages to Buck and to her friends in the Section. With his mouth full of smoked ham, he said he would. It was disquieting to realise that, in a few brief hours, this living being beside her in a French field could pick up a telephone and ask for a number in Essex and be connected and then ask to speak to her children and then talk to them freely. Though she very much wanted to send her love to them, she was silent. By now they would have settled down and become used to her absence and news of her, given by a stranger, would only distress them. It was at that moment that the faint grumble of an aircraft slipped into the silence.

Quickly, Odette collected the remains of the picnic into her rucksack and stood up. Raoul and Paul Frager melted into the half-darkness and Jacques ran along the shadow of the wood to his appointed position. She walked to where the white handkerchief lay on the ground at the angle of the 'L', picked it up, felt the button of her electric torch. The first sound of the Lysander had now swelled to a roar and suddenly, she saw it, skimming in low from the north-east. In the moonlight, she could see a bright light begin to flash and blink as Raoul's lamp gave the 'Q' sign again and again. Dash-dash ... dot ... dash. Dash-dash ... dot ... dash. The Lysander was like a black dragonfly in the sky and its shadow flowed over the field. Right over her head it sped in thunder to disappear beyond the hills. The sound of it grew fainter and fainter and died away. Soon in the quietness she could hear again the cold whisper of wind in the grass.

Raoul turned to Paul Frager. He said in a low voice. 'I don't know what's happened, but she may come back. You'd better lie low here while I warn Lise and Jacques. I'll be back in a moment.'

Stepping lightly on the grass, he walked over to where

Odette stood. He told her to crouch down and wait where she was for ten minutes. If the Lysander hadn't come back by then, she should go to the copse and he would join her. She nodded. He smiled cheerfully and shrugged and tip-toed on to Jacques. Then he went back to Paul and lay down on the freezing ground. Dimly he saw two men cross-ing the field towards him. He nudged Paul and together they pressed their bodies flat to the earth. The two men passed within a few yards, so close that he heard the sharp sound of an iron-shod heel on a stone and the rumble of their voices. They faded into the sheaves of mist and he breathed again.

He heard a distant drone and listened intently. In a moment he was sure. The Lysander was coming back. Quietly he stood up, felt for his torch. The sound of the air-craft rose to *crescendo* and he was just going to flash the 'Q' sign to the sky again when, not 380 yards away, an Aldis lamp suddenly blazed whitely and began to signal the con-trol tower at terrific speed. The trap was sprung.

The meaning of the Aldis lamp signal was immediately clear, for the dark barrack-block burst into light and life. A man's voice shouted furiously in French and Raoul heard every word of his bellowed orders.

'Put out those lights, *imbéciles*. Wait until the plane lands and we'll grab the whole lot!'

There was the sound of confused shouting and the lights in the barrack-block faded into darkness. Steadily and coolly Raoul flashed his agreed dispersal signal towards Odette and Jacques, got a momentary blink of 'message un-derstood'. Then he and Paul Frager broke to the left.

Odette stood stock still for a moment. Though she knew instantly that she was in extreme danger, the beat of her heart was unhurried, and calmly she saw the field, the copse and the river spread out before her like a relief map. She walked lightly towards the edge of the airfield, away from the buildings. Over her head, the Lysander was humming round in circles like an angry hornet and she found time to wish it God-speed and a fair wind to England. Jacques came running up to her and she said: 'You make for the right and I'll meet you on the back road to Perigueux.' He grinned and vanished into the mist. Slowly Odette walked on. The Lysander lifted its wings and soared upwards and away. Quietness fell like rain. She reached the edge of the trees and listened. Then she heard a terrible sound. With a trickle of ice-water spreading over her heart, she knew what that sound meant. It was the savage yelping and whining of a police dog.

She walked a few yards towards the copse and peered into the dim field. She saw or thought she saw a shape like that of a wolf casting, and casting near to where she had stood. With a yelp of triumph, it hit the line and moved towards her, snuffling. She slipped between the trees of the wood and half ran into their dark depths. Once she caught her heel and fell headlong. She heard the dog crash through the freezing bracken and stop. Wide-eyed and scarcely daring to breathe, she got to her feet and moved on into greater darkness. The dog followed and she could hear its body in the undergrowth, coming nearer and nearer. It stopped where she had fallen and whined eagerly, lurched on. Odette stumbled out of the copse and ran swiftly across the moonlit space of grass to the river. It was, she knew with desperation, her last chance and she took it, sliding down the bank and into the freezing water. The coldness of it drove the breath from her body so that she gave a shuddering moan. She waded into the stream and the water rose above her knees to her waist, gripping her cruelly with fingers of ice. The river bed shelved steeply upwards and she plunged through stiff reeds and climbed the far bank, making across a field of frozen stubble to the road. There she stopped to listen and to wring out the dripping hem of her skirt and spill the water out of her shoes. From the airfield, she heard a piercing whistle and the far away sound of a man's voice calling, 'Frizi, Frizi'. With her teeth chattering and her sodden clothes clinging to her, she set out to walk the ten kilometres back to Perigueux.

A few hundred yards down the road, she met Jacques Latour. Two of the four, at any rate, were safe.

When Raoul and Paul Frager had run 100 yards, Paul suddenly stopped. He said that he had left a rucksack where he had been standing and that he was going back for it. He was cool and excited and he said: 'There are twenty beautiful reports in it for Baker Street and we can't leave them for the Gestapo. I'll go back and get it.' He had begun to saunter leisurely back when Raoul overtook him in a sprint and said breathlessly: 'Make for the side of the road and wait for me.' Raoul tore back over the grass, snatched up the rucksack and found Paul who appeared to be taking an almost academic interest in the progress of the chase. Using the cover of the woods and hedges, they made a wide circle to the west and finally settled down in a thicket between half-past three and four in the morning. Both men were used to night work and wore thick clothes. It was well that they did for before dawn, the temperature had sunk to ten degrees below zero. By that time, Raoul's flask of Armagnac was empty and he and Paul were dreamlessly asleep under the stars.

It was about seven o'clock in the morning when Raoul and Paul re-entered Perigueux. As far as was possible, they had tidied themselves up, even to the extent of shaving in a stream by the roadside with the help of a pocket torch. With handfuls of grass, they had cleaned the mud off their shoes. This was of importance. Raoul was reasonably sure that news of last night's happenings would by now have certainly reached both Gestapo and Vichy police in the town and it would be indeed difficult to explain away muddied shoes to a sharp-eyed *flic*. They found a small restaurant and ordered coffee, keeping a sharp eye on the road. By nine o'clock, they had briefly visited every café that was open that Sunday morning. There was still no sign either of Lise or of Jacques, and Raoul, as he chose a table on the terrace of the Grand Hotel overlooking the main square, was conscious of considerable anxiety.

At ten-past nine, Odette walked serenely up the steps of the Grand Hotel. She looked as if she had that moment stepped out of the pages of *Vogue* and she greeted Raoul and Paul with grace. She wore her hat with an air and her frock was immaculate. There were no wrinkles in her silk stockings and the buckles of her high-heeled sandals caught and held the frosty sun. She was followed by Jacques who gave Raoul a cheerful 'Good morning', as he drew up a chair. The four members of the party looked at each other in affectionate silence. Then Raoul's eyes laughed behind their spectacles as he summoned the waitress and said gaily: '*Quatre cafes, s'il vous plaît.*'

Lunch was interesting – and instructive. Not only was the food admirable, but it gave considerable pleasure to Raoul to sit back and listen to four members of the Gestapo at the next table as they discussed the curious goings-on that had been reported from Basillac last night.

'No doubt,' said one of them, 'the swine are still hiding in the woods – if indeed they failed to freeze to death. We shall get them by tonight, never fear, for the cordons are out now beating the coverts.'

'There is a rumour that one of them was a woman.'

'Nonsense, my dear fellow, nonsense. Frenchwomen are not the sort who consent to stay out all night in a freezing field.'

Shortly after this alarming incident at Basillac Raoul and Odette had to leave Cannes because of reports that the Gestapo had put Raoul's apartment under surveillance. They went to Haute Savoie, setting up new headquarters in St Jorioz, a tiny village in the mountains bordering Lake Annecy. Raoul was picked up by a RAF Lysander aircraft for discussions in London. He returned on the night of 14–15 April and landed by parachute on a snow-covered peak in the Alps.

The Nazi net was tightening. The small hotel in St Jorioz was surrounded, and both Raoul and Odette were arrested by the Gestapo. After fruitless interrogations they were handed over to the Abwehr, the German counter-intelligence organisation, and transferred to Fresnes prison in Paris. On the way they managed to have a whispered conversation and for mutual protection decided to pretend that they were married.

Failing to obtain information on the identity of the group's radio operator and on the names of members of the group in the Resistance, the Abwehr sent Odette to the Gestapo for interrogation at the notorious centre at 84, Avenue Foch. She was burned on the spine with a red-hot iron and all her toe-nails wrenched out with pliers. Not only did she refuse to give away names during fourteen sessions of torture, but she obstinately maintained she was married to Raoul, and only at her insistence had he come to France. She agreed that it should be herself and not Raoul who should be shot. As a result Raoul was subjected to only two interrogations, though kept in prison and ultimately sent to a concentration camp.

On 12 May 1944, Odette was transferred to a filthy cell in the criminal prison at Karlsruhe, and then to the extermination camp for women at Ravensbruck. That neither she nor Raoul were executed was largely due to the name Churchill. Raoul (Peter Churchill) was distantly related to the Prime Minister's family, and the Nazis came to accept that Odette was indeed Mrs Peter Churchill. With the Allies storming across the borders of the Reich, the German captors kept their valuable prisoners alive as an insurance policy for their own lives.

The Allied forces liberated them in the final days of the war. Raoul was awarded the DSO and Odette the George Cross.

Notes

[1] Captain Paul Frager, joint commander of the Southern Group. He was later captured and executed.
[2] Colonel M. J. Buckmaster, London chief of SOE.
[3] Marsac End. He and Mme End were captured but survived the war.
[4] Cover name for Captain Alec Rabinovich, executed by the Gestapo in 1944.
[5] Latour was eventually captured, and tortured during interrogation, but survived.

COCKLESHELL HEROES

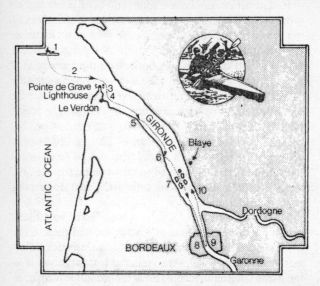

Operation Frankton, later described by the enemy as the outstanding Commando raid of the war, was devised in 1942 to attack Axis merchant ships running the British blockade between German-occupied Bordeaux and the Far East, carrying weapons, machine tools and war equipment to Japan and bringing back crude rubber, ores and edible oils. Bordeaux, Germany's largest port

. KEY TO MAP

1 Launching from submarine 16 km (10 miles) off coast.
2 *Cachalot* damaged on launching.
3 Approximate position *Coalfish* lost and *Conger* capsized.
4 Close to Le Verdon, three German naval craft avoided, then *Cuttlefish* lost.
5 First night, approximately 40 km (25 miles).
6 Second night, approximately 30 km (18.5 miles).
7 Cluster of islets; hiding place by day; 32 km (20 miles).
8 *Catfish* to western bank of Garonne – seven ships as targets.
9 *Crayfish* to eastern bank (no ships) then to Bassens South dock.
10 *Crayfish* and *Catfish* crews land and escape (approximate position).

facility on the Atlantic seaboard, lay far from the sea up the broad estuary of the Gironde and Garonne, every metre of the coast, river banks and port protected by massive air, land and sea defences. Neither airborne nor conventional seaborne attack offered any hope of success, and Vice Admiral Lord Louis Mountbatten, Chief of Combined Operations, authorised the plan to send a dozen Royal Marine Commandos in canoes on a one-way assault to fix limpet mines to the target vessels. After the attack the men would have to escape overland to the Spanish border, some 200 kilometres distant. The canoes, or cockles, were constructed from wood and fabric. They were small enough to be launched from a submarine, but large enough to carry two men with 140 kilograms of equipment, rations, and limpet mines. To avoid detection, the canoes were launched at sea 16 kilometres from the mouth of the Gironde, itself 100 kilometres from the target zone, the distance to be covered inevitably much greater because of strong tides and the need to take evasive action. Movement was to be only at night, with concealment during daylight on the reedy banks and islets, and the journey completed during four nights. Twelve men, including the commander, Major H. G. Hasler, manned six cockles named *Catfish*, *Crayfish*, *Conger*, *Cuttlefish*, *Coalfish* and *Cachalot*. Launching took place late on the evening of 7 December 1942. *Cachalot* was damaged as it was hauled through the submarine hatch and could not proceed. *Coalfish* disappeared in rough water shortly after midnight. The tidal race capsized *Conger*, which could not be righted; its two crewmen were towed by their comrades closer to the river bank in the hope they could struggle ashore. The three surviving canoes carried on, managing to find hiding places at night until they were nearing the port. Then *Cuttlefish* failed to maintain contact with the other two. After darkness on the night of 11-12 December, the limpet mines were fused, the two surviving canoes, *Catfish* and *Crayfish*, prepared to attack.

The weather was again hostile. No rain, no wind, no cloud. A flat calm lay on the waters of the Garonne and all the stars in the heavens looked down at them from a clear, frosty December sky. As *Catfish* stole out, her eight live limpets fizzing away quietly, Hasler was disconcerted to find that, unlike our own blacked-out ports, there were also a great many lights along the banks, including the lights of what appeared to be a factory. He therefore kept *Catfish* about 200 yards off-shore for the greater part of his final approach.

After about ninety minutes' paddling, round a long bend of the Garonne the hunters saw at last their prey. In the distance, moored to the quays on the west bank, some of them brightly illuminated, was a long line of ships. How many, they could not yet count. Hasler and Sparks were filled with elation.

But cunning must still be their precept, for who, in that blaze of lights, could escape detection? Powerful cluster-lamps lit up the decks of several of the ships and the waters around, and lamp-posts were throwing a brilliant light across the entrance to a lock that they would have to pass to starboard before they could put their claws upon the prey. Coming to this lock entrance, *Catfish* swung in a wide arc, then wheeled in again, following the circumference of the lamp's rays.

There was not much time left. The tide was already almost at high-water slack and would be turning against them soon. As they swung away from the lock entrance Hasler had the opportunity he wanted of viewing the ships from a distance, in order to see what types of ships they were; for, as we have seen earlier, once a canoe was close to the towering sides of a big ship, it was impossible to know what she was. He now saw that seven ships lay ready for them — five moored to the quay and two having other vessels moored alongside. Further up the river lay another flock, but it was doubtful if the tide would allow them to get so far. Completing their deviation, Hasler and Sparks brought *Catfish* right up to the quay. Their camouflage hoods were up. From now on they must keep to the deep shadows within a yard of the quay wall or cling close to the water-line of each ship they came upon. They were in single paddles and must use all that they knew of the hunter's wit and cunning.

The first ship was a tanker. She was not their meat and they ignored her, creeping along her hull. Next to her was a liner or cargo liner. They passed her too, but noted her for a kill on the way back if they still had any limpets to spare. Next in the flock was a good cargo ship, but a tanker that was moored alongside made it extremely difficult to get at her. The next ship was a perfect target – a large cargo ship with nothing moored alongside her – and Hasler eagerly prepared to begin putting in his claws. The tide was already beginning to ebb. Just past the bows of the ship he stowed his paddle. Behind him, Sparks, taking up the signal, clung to the ship's side with his magnetic holder, while Hasler reached under his cockpit cover for the first limpet. He attached it to the placing rod. Then he lowered the mine into the water as far as the rod would go, gently brought it up to the ship's side and felt the mine cling. The first blow had been struck.

A few yards on and they were amidships. No alarm yet. No one had heard or seen them. But already Hasler had felt the thrust of the tide against him. He knew he must hand over to Sparks, or the adverse tide would swing the bows of the canoe out and away from the ship's side. Stopping amidships, he therefore passed the placing rod back to his No. 2. Sparks understood at once and gave him the magnetic holder. The roles were reversed and it was now Sparks who dug in the claws. He did so again when Hasler stopped a third time near the ship's stern. That would be enough for this ship.

As they moved along each ship in turn, there was little that they could see except the towering rusty cliff of her side, studded with rivets and pimpled ironically with the real limpets from which their own took its name.

They came to the last ship in the group. They could not

identify her nor get at her properly, for, moored alongside her, was a small German naval craft of the type known as a *sperrbrecher*, about the size of a frigate.

Lurking in the shadows, Hasler sized her up rapidly. She was not the kind of prey he was after – a gazelle among the big water-buck, a pigeon among the fat geese, a mackerel among the sharks. Further upstream he could see another plump herd, but he could never hope to reach them now against the tide. Downstream, on his way back, he knew that there was only one good quarry and that it was difficult to get at. He had five limpets left. He must go home with as full a bag as possible and little fish are sweet. As a German naval vessel, the *sperrbrecher* was anyhow fair game and a justifiable target, so he decided that she should have two limpets. With a few hard strokes *Catfish* was under her bows.

He stopped alongside the German's engine room and there Sparks fixed two limpets spaced several yards apart. Now they must turn to go back downstream, which meant that they must swing out and away into the stream from the ship's side in a wide loop. As they were in the middle of this risky movement, they heard a clang on the ship's deck and a torch shone down on them. A sentry had seen them. His shape was clearly outlined against the night sky as he looked over the rail.

There was only one thing to do. With a cautious drive of the paddles, they slid in right up to the ship's side and froze in the forward low position, hooded heads in their laps. 'I felt,' said Hasler, 'as though my back was stripped naked.'

No shot, no clamour, but the torch still shining down on them from fifteen feet above. Bodies and paddles motionless, they allowed the canoe to drift gently with the tide along the water-line. The sentry, torch in hand, followed them, iron-shod boots clanging on iron deck.

As *Catfish*, like an idle log, drifted down, the *sperrbrecher* seemed to the two Marines to have the length of a battleship and that each clang of the sentry's boots was like the toll of a cracked bell. After an eternity of time, they reached the end of the ship's water-line, drifting in under the flare of her bows, where they were at least invisible from the deck. What now? Go on drifting into the open water beyond and under the glare of the lights? Quietly Hasler handed the magnetic holdfast back to Sparks and made the hold-on signal. With infinite care, Sparks 'rolled' the magnet on the ship's side with a barely audible 'click', and the canoe clung motionless, moored by the stern with the ebb tide running past them to freedom.

When they stopped, the sentry above them stopped too. Presently his torch wandered over the surrounding water, then went out, but he was still there, shifting his feet occasionally. An age passed. No sound of the boots moving away. What was he doing? Waiting for them to show themselves again? Or had he decided they were a piece of driftwood and was taking a rest?

Well, they could not wait for ever. There was another fish to fry. Hasler signalled 'let go' and Sparks removed the holdfast. Without paddling, crouched in the lowest position, they drifted quietly out from under the bows, letting the tide carry them downstream. Once again the agony of waiting for a shot in the back. One minute, two minutes – at last they began to breathe again. They were out of the range of vision and no alarm had been raised. The whole incident was a triumph for those at SOE who had devised this camouflage technique and for the men who had now practised it so convincingly.

Moving quietly on downstream, they passed the ship they had already attacked and came to the awkwardly placed cargo ship, with the tanker moored alongside. Hasler wanted, of course, to distribute his limpets along the length of the merchantman, but the presence of the tanker prevented him from getting at her amidships, so he decided to attack stem and stern. They laid *Catfish* accordingly between the bows of merchantman and tanker and let her glide ahead until she was almost wedged in between them, with the tide now running strongly. Sparks, about to ship his paddle and get out the holder, saw Hasler in front of him suddenly spreadeagle his arms, one on the hull of each ship, as if trying to push them apart. Then he realised that the two ships, yawing slightly under the influence of the tide, were closing together and about to crush the cockle between them. Sparks at once followed suit, and together, pressing with all their strength, they pushed the canoe backwards just in time. 'I felt', said Hasler, 'like Atlas holding up the world.' Back-paddling hard against the tide, they rounded the bows of the tanker and drifted downstream to the stern.

Here they successfully pushed in between the two ships, planting two limpets on the stern end of the cargo ship, spaced as far apart as possible, and the last one on the stern of the tanker.

Their job was done. All their limpets had been successfully planted. The canoe, relieved of the weight of them, suddenly felt lively and unstable. Her crew also felt as though a great weight had been lifted off them. Hasler twisted round in his seat, gripped Sparks's free hand and shook it warmly. They were both smiling for the first time for many hours. Neither of them felt any worries about the dangers of the withdrawal; indeed a kind of quiet recklessness gripped them.

'I felt,' says Hasler, 'as though I owned the river and my respect for the enemy gave way to contempt. I took *Catfish* straight out into the middle of the river, where the tide was strongest, and we shot off downstream, paddling strongly in single paddles. We must have been visible and audible to both banks, if anyone had been looking, but we just didn't seem to care.'

None the less, there was still a great trial to be undergone. Up till now all had been carefully thought out and planned. They had been on the offensive. It was they who, in spite of all obstacles, had controlled events. Now there was no more planning. They would be at the mercy of events. They would have to live by their wits. They were to be no longer soldiers on an organised expedition but refugees in a semi-hostile country. To reach safety, even by the shortest route, they would have to travel at least 800 miles, without transport, or means of subsistence and in the depths of winter.

No such thoughts, however, were in their minds as they made their way again down the Garonne. They thought only of their next purpose, which was to get as far down the estuary as the ebbing tide would carry them before daylight. So, making fast time, they paddled past their last hide, past the two ships at Bassens South that had been allotted as Laver's victims. Then, too early for safety, they changed to double paddles and really began to move, sweeping past the sleeping villages and the tall, silent reeds, till they came almost back again to the scene of that disagreeable hide on the Ile de Cazeau and once more turned off the main channel to pass inside the islands. Here they stopped in midstream for a rest, drifting idly along with the tide in the utter stillness.

Presently they heard a faint but familiar noise astern of them, rapidly getting louder. 'It sounded,' says Hasler, 'like a Mississippi stern-wheeler at full speed, but we knew what it was and we laughed aloud.' Turning *Catfish* round, they soon saw the shape of a canoe materialise out of the darkness, travelling fast in double paddles 'with a bone in her teeth'. Suddenly the paddling stopped, and the oncoming canoe 'froze'. They had just spotted the stationary *Catfish*, but were not close enough to identify her. 'Good work, Laver,' thought Hasler. The cry of a very cautious seagull whispered over the water and Hasler, laughing aloud in the height of his spirits, sent back an answer that sounded like a seagull in the summit of intoxication.

Instantaneously, the other canoe 'unfroze' and paddled swiftly up. It was Corporal Laver. They rafted up together joyfully, Laver and Mills in great spirits.

'We went right down the east bank as far as we could, sir, like you said,' Laver whispered to Hasler, 'until the tide turned against us, and we found no targets at all. So we came back and attacked the two ships at Bassens South.'

'Well done. What did you give them?'

'Five limpets on the first ship, sir, and three on the second.'

'Meet any trouble?'

'None at all, sir. All went off much better than "Blanket".'

'Just as well for both of us. Anyhow, well done indeed you two. And' – turning round to his own No. 2 – 'well done, Sparks. You've all done wonderfully, and I'm really proud of you.'

For a few more minutes the two canoes lay together, while the men whispered and laughed silently. Then Hasler said that it was time for them to separate and withdraw independently, as laid down in the orders. Laver said: 'Couldn't we go along with you for a bit, sir? It would be nice to keep company as long as we could.' 'All right,' Hasler answered, 'if you would like to. But we shall have to separate before we land.'

So, united again, *Catfish* and *Crayfish* assumed their wonted stations for their last passage, sweeping back into the Gironde, through the narrow waters between the Ile de Cazeau and the mainland, driving the canoes as fast as they would go, for they wanted to put as much distance as possible between themselves and Bordeaux before the excitement began. As always, the tide was the determining factor. Once the flood stream turned against them, they would be forced to land or be swept back upstream.

Hasler therefore turned away to starboard, crossed the shipping channel to the east bank and slipped past the sleeping town of Blaye. Here, lying opposite Blaye, they passed the big French liner *De Grasse*, at anchor and with no sign of life on board, Hasler knew, from his Intelligence briefing, that she was laid up for the duration of the war. One day she would set out once again on her familiar track to New York, and he wished her good luck.

A little north of Blaye the little party stopped and looked back. There, a few miles away, from the direction of the point where the Garonne and the Dordogne meet, a searchlight was sweeping the estuary; perhaps it was as well that they had avoided the main channel.

It was now six o'clock in the morning, only an hour and a half before dawn, and the flood tide had already begun to turn against them. But they had got far enough to be able to land in open country to the north of Blaye, with a clear escape route to the north-east. For five successive nights the two canoes had been at large in enemy waters, covering a total of 91 sea miles, or 105 land miles, by canoe alone. Their cockles had proved themselves.

For the last time, Hasler made the 'raft-up' signal. As Laver and Mills came alongside he said: 'Well, Corporal, this is where we have to separate. You are about a mile north of Blaye. Go straight ashore here and carry out your escape instructions. I shall land about a quarter of a mile further north.'

Laver looked at him steadily and said:

'Very good, sir. Best of luck to you.'

For him it was perhaps an even harder moment than the time, nine hours before, when they had separated for the attack. Now, a young fellow of twenty-two, without superior schooling, he would have to land in a completely strange and semi-hostile country, knowing nothing of the language, and use his own wits to get through, venturing into the unknown without guide or leader. It would have been a lot to ask of an officer, but Corporal Laver did not shrink from it.

'Goodbye, both of you,' said Hasler, 'and thank you for everything you've done. Keep on as you've been doing and we'll be meeting again in Pompey in a few weeks' time.'

Reaching across the gunwales, they shook hands all round, each with a 'Good luck!' for the other. But it was Sparks who struck the right note at the final moment.

'See you in the "Granada",' he said with his infectious smile. 'We'll keep a couple of pints for you!'

So it was with a quiet laugh that they pushed the canoes away from each other and paddled away on their separate courses. Just once Hasler looked back over his right shoulder at *Crayfish*, paddling strongly for the shore. She looked to him suddenly very small, very helpless, and he quickly looked away again. For a moment his heart was heavy, as it had been when he said goodbye to Sheard and

Moffat, and it was with an effort that he forced himself to concentrate on the problem of landing.

It was the last they ever saw of the gallant Laver and Mills.

The limpet mines exploded at intervals during the morning of 12 December. Seven ships were sunk or severely damaged. The enemy was completely mystified, suspecting drifting mines or sabotage by the French Underground, until the abandoned *Crayfish* and *Catfish* were found downstream, where the four crew members had landed to make their escape. Hasler and Sparks, periodically given food and shelter by French civilians, were eventually put in contact with the famous English-born 'Marie-Claire' and her son Marcel, who hid them in a safe house near Lyon until they could be guided to the Spanish border. They crossed the Pyrenees at the end of February and reached British territory in Gibraltar on 1 April 1943. Laver and Mills, from *Crayfish*, were picked up after two days' walking inland by the French police and handed over to the Germans. Mackinnon and Conway in *Cuttlefish*, who had lost contact with the other two surviving canoes, carried out their mission until their canoe was damaged. They apparently got ashore and evaded capture for two weeks, but were betrayed by an informer. Wallace and Ewart, the crew of *Coalfish*, missing during the first night of the operation, were taken prisoner on 8 December. The body of Moffat, who had been towed towards the shore by his comrades after *Conger* capsized, was washed up on 17 December; his fellow crew member, Sheard, was never found. On the express orders of Hitler, furious at the successful assault on the 'impregnable port of Bordeaux', the prisoners were shot after interrogation, despite the fact that they were in uniform with Royal Marines insignia. The burial certificates stated that they had all been 'found drowned in Bordeaux harbour'.

THE WOODEN HORSE

One of the most courageous and ingenious plans for escape from a German prison camp during the Second World War involved the construction of a twentieth-century Trojan horse – in this instance a wooden vaulting horse built from odd pieces of timber and carried out each day for gymnastics by the prisoners.

Beneath the horse was the opening to a tunnel slowly excavated in the sandy sub-soil. It burrowed below the open ground surrounding the prison huts, underneath the double fences, watch towers, arc lamps and trip wires, and avoided the buried sound sensors. Beyond the prison lay the pine forest and some semblance of freedom, though, of course, still deep in enemy territory.

Stalag Luft III, built with maximum security to hold the Nazis' most prized prisoners of war, was at Sagan, in thinly populated country on the borders of the Reich and occupied Poland, far from the Baltic Sea, the only practicable route to freedom.

With incredible patience the tunnellers scooped away the soil, hauling it back in a basin to the opening beneath the horse, over which other prisoners kept up their interminable exercises. The soil was put in bags hung inside the horse, and the prisoners smuggled out the bags and dispersed the soil later. Week after week went by during that hot summer of 1943 until at last, on 29 October, the tunnel, just large enough for a man to lie prone and wriggle forward, stretched nearly 40 metres and was ready for the escape.

When Eric Williams wrote his book *The Wooden Horse* security regulations prohibited the use of the actual names of the men involved. Peter Howard is the fictional name of the author. He was an RAF Flight Lieutenant shot down during a bombing raid on Duisburg in the Ruhr in December, 1942. John Clinton in the story is Captain Michael Codner, Royal Artillery, taken prisoner in North Africa. Flight Lieutenant Oliver Philpot, of the RAF, shot down at the end of 1941, appears in the story as Philip Rowe.

The prisoners used many slang terms. German guards were goons. Special guards, employed to watch for escape attempts, were ferrets. The prisoners themselves were kriegies.

For the next twelve days there was an Indian summer, and they were able to take the horse out every morning and afternoon. Working up to a crescendo of effort they dug faster and increased the number of bags to be carried back at a time from twelve to fourteen and finally fifteen. With the extra weight the bearers were beginning to stagger as they carried the horse up the steps into the canteen; and Peter wondered how they would cope when they had three men inside. The smallest and lightest of the regular vaulters was a New Zealander called McKay. When they asked if he would come out and close the trap after them he agreed immediately.

They decided to break on Friday 29 October. The work

went so well that they had time to make a final bulge where John would stow the baggage. They dug the bulge on the 28th; it was as far as they could go. They reckoned that between them they could dig a further ten feet after they had been sealed down the next evening.

On the morning of the 29th they brought in the second batch of fifteen bags, and recovered their civilian clothing from scattered hiding places round the camp. Ralph, the Committee Clothing Officer, handed over the phoney Marine dress uniform; to his evident satisfaction and Peter's relief, it proved a good fit. When he had removed the tacked-on stripes from the trouser-legs, the patch pockets, and the epaulettes and insignia from the shoulders, it became an almost-too-good civilian suit for a foreign worker to wear in wartime Germany.

With all their gear mustered and checked, they packed it into kitbags and took them to the canteen, hidden in bundles of other kriegies' dirty laundry.

At 12.30 John had a substantial meal of bully beef and potatoes, Canadian biscuits and cheese. At 1 p.m., wearing his civilian shirt and trousers under a long khaki greatcoat, he left for the canteen with the male voice choir. Peter hurried off to see the duty pilot, who told him there were two ferrets in the compound.

'Where are they?'

'One's in the kitchen, and Charlie's [the chief ferret] hanging around outside the canteen.'

'Hell!' Peter thought for a moment. 'OK – if any more come into the compound send a stooge off to tell Phil. He'll be in the canteen.'

He ran across to the hut where the SBO [Senior British Officer] lived; and knocked on his door.

'Come in.'

He stood in the doorway, panting slightly. 'Sir – we're just putting Clinton down and Charlie's hanging round the canteen. I wonder if you could get him out of the way for a few minutes?'

'Let me see.' The Group Captain put down his book.

'The cooking stove in Hut 64 isn't working very well. I'll just stroll over and ask him to report it to the Kommandantur. He might like to smoke an English cigarette with me.'

Back at the canteen Peter found the choir lustily singing 'Greensleeves'. John, Philip, Nigel and the vaulting team were standing near the door.

'Can't get started,' John said. 'Charlie's outside and he keeps walking past and looking in at the window. I think he likes the singing.'

'Let's change it to "Run, rabbit, run"!' Nigel suggested.

'There's another ferret next door in the kitchen,' Peter said. 'The SBO's going to take Charlie away —'

'I'll deal with the one in the kitchen.' It was Winyard, whose Vorlager *dienst* had not yet broken, come to see John off.

'Fine,' Peter said. 'Then we'll get cracking.' He looked out of the window. The SBO was walking across the compound, a golf club in his hand. Suddenly he appeared to see Charlie, and altered course. 'Here comes Groupy.'

The Group Captain and Charlie exchanged a few words and they both walked away towards Hut 64. They could hear Tony Winyard chatting with the ferret in the kitchen. Hurriedly John doffed his coat and pulled the long black combinations on over his shirt and trousers. He pulled black socks over his shoes and a hood which he had made from an old undervest dyed black over his head. 'It's bloody hot in this clobber,' he whispered.

'You look like the Ku Klux Klan,' Peter said, 'Ready?'

With the choir singing more loudly than ever, they both crawled under the vaulting horse; Peter holding a blanket, a cardboard box and fifteen empty bags, John sinister in his black outfit. The three kitbags hung between them, suspended on hooks wedged under the top of the horse. They crouched with their backs to the ends of the horse, their feet one each side on the bottom framework. Then the bearing poles were inserted and the horse was lifted. As they lurched down the steps and went creaking across the compound towards the vaulting pits, they held on to the kitbags to prevent them from falling off the hooks.

With a sigh of relief the bearers placed the horse in position and withdrew the poles. The vaulting began.

John crouched in one end of the horse while Peter piled the kitbags on top of him. Peter then spread the blankets on the ground at the other end and began to uncover the trap. He collected the top layer of grey sand in the cardboard box, and threw the damp subsoil on to the blanket. Feeling round with his fingers he uncovered the bags of sand on top of the trap and removed them. He scraped the remaining sand away from the damp wood. As he lifted the trap he smelled the familiar damp mustiness of the tunnel. He lifted the kitbags off John's crouching figure and balanced them on top of the trap on the pile of sand.

'Down you go.' He crouched astride the hole while John dropped feet first into the shaft. 'Those clothes stink!'

'It'll be worse by the time you come down,' John said. 'It's the dye. Must have gone bad or something.'

As John crawled up the tunnel Peter detached the metal basin from the end of the rope and tied one of the kitbags in its place. One by one John pulled the kitbags up to the face and stowed them in the bulge. Peter then re-tied the basin, and John sent back enough sand to fill the empty bags.

While Peter was stacking the bags in the body of the horse, John crawled back for his last breath of fresh air. It was the first time he had been in the tunnel wearing clothes and Peter could hear him cursing softly as he struggled to get back. His feet came into view and then his body, clothed and clumsy in the black combinations. Peter crouched inside the horse looking down on him as he emerged. The shouting of the vaulters outside and the reverberating concussion as they landed on the canvas padding above his head seemed louder than usual.

John straightened up, head and shoulders out of the trap. He had left the hood at the end of the tunnel and his face was flushed. He looked strange with short hair; smaller, older. 'It's hot down there with clothes on.'

'Take it easy,' Peter said. 'For Christ's sake don't overdo

it. I don't want to have to carry you once we get outside.'

'I'll be all right. You seal me down now and I'll see you after *appell*.'

'OK – don't make the air hole bigger than you have to.'

He watched John's feet disappear down the narrow tunnel and then he closed the trap. He replaced the heavy bags of sand over it and stamped the loose sand firmly on top of them. He didn't like doing it. It's burying a man alive, he thought. He heard an urgent voice from outside.

'How's it going, Pete?'

'Five minutes, Phil.'

He started to hang the fifteen bags full of sand from the top of the horse. He gathered the blanket in his arms and spread the rest of the sand evenly over the ground under the horse. He sprinkled the dry grey sand from the cardboard box over this, and smoothed it carefully. Finally he gave Philip a low hail that he was ready. The bearing poles were inserted and he was carried back towards the canteen. He could hear the voices of the choir: '*He shall give His angels charge over thee ... lest thou dash thy foot against a stone. ...*' In the dark belly of the horse he laughed softly, releasing tension.

With a last creaking lurch they were up the steps and inside. The old horse is falling to pieces, he thought; hope it lasts out this evening.

One end was lifted. Before crawling out he passed the bags of sand to Philip. They began to carry the bags into the band practice room where the choir was going at full blast.

'*... the young lion and the dragon ... there's a ferret passing the window*,' sang David.

'There bloody well would be,' Peter said. 'Keep an eye on him. Is Nig in the roof?'

David nodded and went on singing, '*... because He hath known my name. ...*'

'Right – we'll just pass these bags up to him and then we're in the clear.'

Nigel's anxious face was peering down from the trapdoor in the ceiling. Peter held out his fist, thumb extended upwards, and grinned. Nigel grinned back, and lowered his hand for the first of the bags.

'. . . *with long life will I satisfy Him*. . . .'

Back in the mess Peter first trimmed, then shaved off his beard. In the mirror he had made from a smoothed-out Klim tin and nailed to his bunk, he watched his features emerge, round and unlined. John had looked years older with cropped hair. Without his thick wiry black beard he himself looked younger than his thirty-two years, innocent and inexperienced. Somehow, discarding the beard was his final commitment to the escape; and he was impatient to get on with it. This two hours' wait with John sealed down the tunnel was going to be the worst time of all. It was touch and go now. At any moment until they reached the shelter of the trees the scheme might be blown. At any moment the four-and-a-half months of back-breaking effort might go for a Burton.

Stretched out on his bunk he stopped worrying while he wondered about the origins of 'gone for a Burton'. Airmen used the phrase, or said 'bought it', as euphemisms when fellow airmen were killed. Both must have stemmed from that brewers' advertisement *Where's George? Gone for a Burton*. What would the first beer taste like? He turned his thoughts back to the escape. Once they were outside it wouldn't matter so much; it was the next few hours that mattered. Outside anything might happen, and they would have to rely almost entirely on luck. It was no use making detailed plans like they'd done for the tunnel. They had a rough idea of what they wanted to do – get to Stettin and board a Swedish ship – but that was all. From the moment they broke out of the tunnel they would have to adapt their actions, maybe their policy, to the conditions and even the people they met.

Always reluctant to ponder imponderables, he let his mind run over the list of things he was taking with him. There was the 'dog food', a hard cake made from dried milk, sugar, Bemax and cocoa; it had been packed in small square tins saved from the Red Cross parcels, and he intended to wear a girdle of them under his shirt. Next there were the linen bags containing a dry mixture of oatmeal, raisins, sugar and milk powder; mixed with water it would swell and fill the stomach, preventing that hollow aching sickness that comes from eating ill-balanced, concentrated food. He had sewn one of these bags into each armpit of his trench coat as emergency rations in case they were separated from the attaché-case which held the bulk of their food.

The attaché-case was already down in the tunnel, at the bottom of his kitbag. Mentally he re-checked its contents: the food, clean socks, shaving gear, rollneck sweater, soap, a few sheets of paper, and pen and ink for minor alterations to their documents. German cigarettes and matches.

He got to his feet and went through his jacket pockets: the wallet which held the papers and the Reichsmarks, the pocket compass and torch supplied by the Committee, two handkerchiefs, cigarettes bought in the town by one of the tame guards, a length of string, a pencil, a pen-knife, his beret and a comb.

It was no use, he couldn't be still. He went out on the circuit and walked round, over the tunnel; thinking of John moling away down there, sweating, not knowing the time, not knowing whether the tunnel had been discovered, out of touch with everyone. John digging away, trying to get as much done as possible before he and Philip joined him.

He went unnecessarily to the abort, checked with Philip on the timing of the diversion for the break, and then walked with Nigel round and round the circuit while they waited for *appell.*

Nigel broke a long silence. 'David and I . . .' he hesitated, diffident. 'We thought we'd have a bash at the tunnel tomorrow – that's if you don't mind. The chaps could take us out after lunch and we'd stay down there until dark.'

'But – what about your leg? We wanted to ask you to come in with us – before we asked Phil. But we thought —'

'I know,' Nigel said. 'John told me. I'm glad you didn't. I'd only have held you up. And Phil deserves it.'

'Are you and David going together?'

'Oh no – I'd hold him up too. I'm going as a discharged soldier – dumb from shellshock as well as wounded. Hitching lifts on my way home to Bavaria from the *Ostfront*. I'll try to get into Switzerland if I get that far. They've got the papers ready. David's jumping goods trains – heading for France.'

'Well, jolly good luck to you both,' Peter said.

'I just wanted to know . . .' he hesitated again, 'to ask whether you could camouflage the hole a bit before you leave.'

Peter could see the complication, the necessity to stay there in the light of the arc-lamps; but Nigel deserved the chance. David too. 'I'm second man out,' he said. 'Phil's the last. It rather depends on how far we can mole. If we come out in the ditch we might manage it.'

'We don't want to jeopardize your effort,' Nigel said. 'We just thought —'

'I'll talk to Phil. You have everything ready in any case. Even if we can't cover the hole there's always the outside chance. The ghosts'll take our places at morning *appell* so if the hole hasn't been seen by then you've got a chance.' If it's not been discovered by then, he thought, we shall be well on our way.

'I don't expect I shall get far,' Nigel said. 'nowhere near any of the Death Zones.[1] But I'd like to have a bash . . . I shall miss you after you've gone. It's been good fun, the vaulting.'

'I expect they'll take the horse away when they discover the tunnel,' Peter said. He wanted to thank Nigel for all the help and encouragement he'd given them, but he knew that he could not do it. To thank him in words would put the thing on a formal basis and it was beyond that.

'You will see my wife, Pete?'

'First thing when I get home. Don't take any risks, will you, Nig?'

'You know me,' Nigel replied. 'I'm dumb enough to forget I'm dumb and yell "Goon in the block!" when I see my first policeman.'

With *appell* safely over, the vaulters assembled in the canteen for the third time that day. Peter's knees felt loose and for a moment he did not want to get into the horse. He felt that three was an unlucky number, that the guards in the watch-towers were bound to be suspicious when they saw the horse being brought out again, after the evening *appell*.

The moment passed and he wanted to get on with it, quickly. As he pulled on the evil-smelling black combinations, he heard Nigel instructing the four men who were to carry the horse. He looked at Philip, unrecognisable in his black hood; and then at the third man, McKay, stripped for lightness and holding the cardboard box ready for the dry surface sand which he would sprinkle over the bags on the trap after he had sealed them down.

Nigel came over and handed him a bottle of cold tea for John. 'Give the child my love,' he said, 'and tell him to write.' He turned abruptly and limped over to the window.

Peter and Philip crawled under the horse, stood crouching one at each end, and held McKay suspended between them. The bearer poles were pushed into position and they braced themselves on these. The four men lifted the horse. It creaked protestingly and seemed to Peter to sag in the middle. One of the bearers slipped as they came down the steps; recovered his balance; and the horse went swaying and jerking across the football pitch.

Once the horse was in position over the shaft Philip sat on McKay's back at one end while Peter removed the trap. As he lifted the wooden boards he listened for sounds of movement at the end of the tunnel. It was silent. He turned to Philip.

'I'll carry on up the tunnel and see how John's doing. You fill some bags from the bottom of the shaft for Kiwi to take back, and then stay down this end. I'll send the stuff John's dug back in the basin and you leave as much as you can this end, then spread the rest along the floor of the tunnel.'

'Right. It's 16.05 now.' Philip was looking at the Rolex

wristwatch he had borrowed from a member of his mess. 'We'd better get cracking.'

Peter dropped feet first into the vertical shaft. McKay, stoically silent in the discomfort of the journey from the canteen, eased out from under Philip and spoke at last.

'My bloody oath!' He was staring in wonder down at the tunnel entrance. 'Is it as small as that all the way?'

'Smaller.' Peter slid to his knees, edging his legs and feet into the back burrow. 'Thanks a lot, Kiwi. Don't forget to smooth the surface sand —'

'My bloody oath! Good luck, mate.'

Stooping awkwardly in his tight clothing Peter managed to get his head under the lintel of the opening and slipped head first into the tunnel. He waved his legs in farewell, and squirmed inch by inch along the 100 feet that had taken them so long to dig. Now that it was finished and he was crawling down it for the last time, he was almost sorry.

He switched on the torch. Stafford had been right about the battery. Even so, it was a help. As he inched forward he could see heaps of loose sand dislodged by John's clothing. He noticed all the patches of shoring, built with difficulty in darkness, strangely unfamiliar in the light. Near the end of the tunnel he flashed the torch ahead and called softly to John. He was afraid to call loudly for he was now under the wire and not far from one of the watch-towers.

He came to the bend where they had altered course, and saw the end of the tunnel. Where he had expected to find John there was nothing but a solid wall of sand.

John must have been digging on steadily and, banking up the sand behind him, had completely blocked the tunnel.

Peter began to bore through the wall of loose sand. After about three feet he broke through. A gust of hot fetid air gushed out; and there was John, sweat- and sand-covered, hands and face streaked with black dye. A fringe of hair, wet and caked with sand, plastered his forehead. He looked pale and exhausted in the yellow light of Peter's torch.

'Where the bloody hell have you been?' he asked.

'It's not 4.30 yet.'

'I thought it must have gone six. I seem to have been down here for ever. I thought the roll-call had gone wrong and I'd have to go out alone.'

'Everything's under control,' Peter said. 'Nig sent you some tea, with his love.' He pushed the bottle through. 'I'll just get this sand back to Phil and then I'll join you.'

He pulled the empty basin up the tunnel and sent the first load back to Phil, who filled the empty bags they had brought out and stacked them in the shaft. When all twelve were ready he hung them in the horse, and gave McKay the word to replace the trap and seal them in.

As Peter and John worked on they had a certain amount of fresh air from the air hole under the wire. Philip, back in the vertical shaft with the trap closed above him, had none. When he found himself gasping for breath he crawled up the tunnel and joined in the moling.

They worked feverishly, trying to get as much as possible done before the breaking time. John, in front, stabbed at the face with the trowel and pushed the damp sand under his belly towards Peter, who lay with his head on John's heels collecting the sand and squirmed backwards with it to Philip, who banked it up as a wall behind them. They were now in a narrow stretch of the tunnel about twenty-five feet long and two feet square, ventilated by one small hole three inches in diameter.

They were working for the first time in clothes and for the first time without the fresh air pushed up the tunnel from the open shaft by the movement of the basin. They were working three in the tunnel and they were anxious about the air; Peter and Philip especially, because they knew from flying how lack of oxygen could create a sense of euphoria so that a man got careless and made stupid mistakes. They were working for the first time by the light of a torch, and in the light the tunnel seemed smaller and the earth above more solid. By now the prisoners had been locked in their huts for the night. If the tunnel collapsed the three of them would be helpless.

They worked fast, steadily yet silently. None of them

wanted to be the one to break the rhythm of the work.

At 5.30 Peter called a halt. 'Half an hour to go,' he whispered. 'We'd better push up to the top.'

John nodded his agreement, and began to push the tunnel uphill, towards the surface. It proved farther than they had expected and they thought they would never get there. Then John broke through – a hole as large as his fist. Through it he caught his first glimpse of the stars. The stars in the free heavens beyond the wire.

'I'll dig out the whole width of the tunnel,' he whispered, 'just leaving a thin crust over the top. Then we can break that quickly, at six o'clock exactly. There'll be less risk of being seen while we wait.'

Peter gripped his ankle in reply and squirmed back to Philip to warn him to get ready. He retrieved John's kitbag from the third bulge, pushed it ahead of him up the tunnel, and tied it to John's ankle. He returned to the bulge, extracted his own bag, and got Philip to do the same for him. He dragged it behind him towards the mouth of the tunnel where John was resting. Philip followed, pushing his own gear ahead of him, in front of his nose. It was 5.30, and they were ready.

At 6 p.m. John broke through to the open air, pulling the dry sandy surface down, choking and blinding himself and making him want to cough. As the sand settled they heard the sound of the diversion coming from the huts nearest the wire. There were men blowing trumpets, men singing 'My Brother Sylveste', men banging the sides of the hut and yelling at the top of their voices.

'They're overdoing it,' John whispered. 'The silly bastards'll get a bullet in there if they're not careful.'

'Go on! Go now!' Peter said. He was scared. It was too light. The hole was some feet short of the ditch, on the edge of the outside sentry's path.

John hoisted his kitbag out of the tunnel and rolled it towards the ditch. He squeezed himself up out of the hole and disappeared from view.

Peter stuck his head out of the tunnel. He looked towards

the camp. It was brilliantly floodlit, he had not realised how brilliantly. The high watch-towers were in darkness and he could not see whether the guards were looking into the camp, at the noisy huts, or in his direction. He pulled out his kitbag and pushed it into the ditch, wriggled out of the hole and dragged himself full-length across the open ground and into the ditch. He expected every second to hear the crack of a rifle and feel the tearing impact of its bullet in his flesh. He lay, out of breath, in the shallow ditch and looked back.

The hole was in the full light of the arc-lamps. It would be impossible for Phil to stay and cover it.

The diversion in the huts reached a new crescendo of noise. He picked up his kitbag and ran blindly across the road, into the pine forest where John was waiting.

Once they reached the shelter of the trees they did not wait for Philip but walked slowly on, away from the wire. Peter could feel his heart thumping high up inside his chest. He wanted to run but he forced himself to walk slowly and carefully, feeling with his feet for the brittle dry branches and pine cones that lay among the needles on the forest floor. His tunnelling clothes were wet with perspiration and the keen night wind cut through them. He was cold, but they must get deeper into the forest before they could dress.

They heard no shots and knew that Philip too must have gained the safety of the trees unseen.

Peter stopped behind a big pine, leaned his kitbag against the trunk and looked back at the camp, floodlit like some gigantic empty stadium.

'Come on, Pete,' John whispered. 'We'll have to move if we're going to catch that train.'

But Peter stood for a moment longer gazing at the compound that he knew so well; the wire that he hated, the huts which held so many of his friends.

'*Come on!*'

As they walked deeper into the forest, John began to laugh under his breath, giggling at first, then shaking with long gusts of low uncontrollable mirth.

'What the hell's the matter?' Peter whispered. 'What the

hell are you laughing at?'

'It's you,' John said, gasping, 'you look like some great mother bear mincing along carrying a baby. . . .'

'Bloody funny.' But he too was laughing; laughing with the release of strained nerves and the triumph of escape. Lying at the end of the tunnel, waiting for the diversion, he'd thought they would never make it across the road and into the forest in the full light of the arc-lamps, the full view of the watch-towers. Now they'd done that he began to think that everything was possible, that they'd make it all the way. Such confidence was dangerous, he must watch it.

'Let's get out of these combinations,' John said. 'Get cleaned up and dressed like human beings.'

'Not yet. Lay the trail away from the railway station. We'll hide them near the side of the road to Breslau.'

Now they threaded their way between the trees on a route parallel to the camp, using the lights as direction beacons.

'I'm bloody cold.' John was trembling with a mixture of cold and fatigue.

'So am I. Not much farther.' He realised that John must be exhausted after all the moling, and that he still had the task of buying tickets ahead of him. It would have been good to spend the night in the forest and catch an early train; but they could not risk it. They must press on this evening and put miles between themselves and the camp before the alarm was given. With the tunnel exit so near the sentry's path there was no chance it would not be seen.

When he judged they were about a mile from the station Peter called a halt. He looked at his watch. 6.12; about right – they would not have too long to wait for the train.

Quickly they stripped off the black combinations and the socks from their shoes. They washed one another's faces with their handkerchiefs and took their civilian jackets, berets and mackintoshes from the kitbags.

At the bottom of the kitbags they had each packed a small travelling bag. Peter opened his, a fibre attaché-case, and took out a tin of pepper. He put the combinations, socks, hoods and kitbags together in a heap and sprinkled them liberally with the pepper, holding his nose to prevent himself sneezing.

Fully dressed in suits, mackintoshes and berets they doubled back towards the railway, making straight for the bridge that led to the station, a high metal footbridge which crossed the line. They gained the road on the far side.

'Let's keep to the right,' Peter said, 'then we shan't be facing oncoming traffic.'

They met several people on the road. A local train had evidently just pulled in. Hope to God they're not waiting at the station, Peter thought; hope the alarm hasn't gone and we don't find a posse of guards waiting for us.

'If we're recognised we'll cut and run,' he said. 'They won't shoot with all these people about. We'll separate. I'll meet you by the water tower in the forest. Then we'll walk. Once they know we're out all the stations for miles around will be alerted.'

'It's OK.' Warmer, cleaner and properly dressed, John was keyed up for the journey. 'If the alarm had gone we'd have heard it. We'll catch the train all right.'

They did – the first of many stages on the long journey across eastern Germany through Frankfurt-on-Oder and the Nazi military strongpoint of Kustrin (now Kostrzyn) to the Baltic port of Stettin (now Szczecin). Posing as Frenchmen conscripted for forced labour, they found that their forged identity cards and travel permits were accepted without suspicion by railway officials and police. When the small amount of food they had brought with them gave out they were forced to risk entering cafés and canteens for a cup of ersatz coffee and the rudimentary meal obtainable without ration coupons. Often they had to sleep rough, but in order to maintain some semblance of normal appearance they chanced staying in cheap hotels for foreign workers.

The military guards and civil police around the heavily protected harbour zone of Stettin brought even greater danger, but thanks to the courageous help of French conscripts working in the docks John and Peter were able to contact the crew of a Danish freighter due to sail for Copenhagen and Oslo. En route the ship would briefly pass through neutral waters off the Swedish coast. The crew managed to hide the stowaways during the search by German troops and the Gestapo, and the ship put out to sea. It seemed escape had been achieved – only to find that German naval vessels were shadowing the freighter. The choice was either to jump ship under cover of darkness and swim a mile through icy seas to the safety of Sweden or remain hidden on the ship till it reached Copenhagen. Inevitably they chose the latter course. In Copenhagen they were hidden in a safehouse until the ship was once more ready to sail, this time with stores for the German troops in Norway. Once again the Germans made a futile search (it was learned later that an informer had told the Gestapo that stowaways were on board). At last the ship steered just within the three-mile limit from the Swedish coast. A Swedish patrol boat hove to beside it and its captain courteously enquired if there were any passengers wishing to come ashore.

Philip, the third man to escape from the tunnel, had chosen to travel alone, disguised as a Norwegian business man. He also used trains to cross Germany, managing to reach Danzig (now Gdansk) in under twenty-four hours. He found a neutral ship bound for Sweden and met Peter and John when they arrived in Stockholm.

Philip was flown home first. On 28 December, nine weeks after Peter and John dropped into the tunnel below the Wooden Horse they were in an RAF Dakota bound for Scotland.

Note

[1] A notice posted in the camp warned that Germany had created Death Zones around industrial and military areas in which all unauthorised trespassers would be shot on sight.

THE ARREST OF THE WHITE RABBIT

None of the British agents who operated in Occupied France during the Second World War played such a vital role and subsequently endured such prolonged and appalling torture at the hands of the Gestapo as Forest Frederick Edward Yeo-Thomas. Born in England in 1901, he was educated in France. When war broke out he was a director of Molyneux, the Parisian fashion house. He enlisted in the RAF, becoming an interpreter, until joining the Free French section of Special Operations Executive.

Fluent in French, and with deep knowledge both of the country and the people, Yeo-Thomas became the key man in the links between French patriots and Britain. By parachute or Lysander aircraft he went to France on his mission to weld the five main Resistance groups, plus a host of smaller units, into a secret army. He organised the recruiting and transport of agents, the deliveries of arms, money, medical supplies, and food to selected sites, and set up a reliable communications network, with 'safe houses' all over the country. On one quick trip to Britain he personally persuaded Churchill to order 100 aircraft, flying 250 sorties a month, to maintain the supplies and land and pick up agents.

He had many identities, complete with the necessary identification papers. In the coded messages broadcast by the BBC he was *Le Petit Lapin Blanc* (The Little White Rabbit).

The Nazis were aware of a master mind at work. They branded Yeo-Thomas as 'a dangerous terrorist to be exterminated'. In the Paris region alone 32 000 agents searched for Shelley, as they knew him. Arrest after arrest of men and women in the Resistance made the risk of information being extracted under torture more acute. While on a routine trip for briefing in London Yeo-Thomas learned that two of his closest French comrades, Brossolette and Bollaert, had been caught by the Gestapo in Brittany as they were attempting to get to England by boat. On the night of 24 February 1944, Yeo-Thomas, accompanied by a saboteur named Trieur, took off from Tempsford airfield, near Bedford, with further orders for sabotage and preparation for the Allies' invasion of France. Yeo-Thomas made a personal pledge to himself: he would attempt the rescue of Brossolette and Bollaert from Rennes prison before they were tortured and executed.

Because of the necessity for rescuing Brossolette before his identity was discovered Tommy had elected to jump in the dark rather than wait for the next moon period. He was accompanied by a saboteur whose code name was Trieur and whose first trip this was.

They were to be dropped near Clermont-Ferrand, about 250 miles south of Paris, and had a long way to fly. There was the usual flak over the French coast, but the rest of the journey passed without incident.

The procedure was the same as on his first mission with

Passy[1] and Brossolette: when they were nearly over the pin-point the dispatcher hooked up their static lines and opened up the hole. Trieur looked nervous and Yeo-Thomas, who was to jump first, tried to cheer him up by giving him the thumbs-up sign as he swung his legs into the trap. Below it was inky black and it was some time before Tommy could see the twinkling lights of the reception committee. Then he felt the dispatcher's hand on his shoulders, the red light went on, the aircraft made a wide turn and ran in over the ground; the green light went on, he pushed himself out through the hole, whirled round in the slipstream, floated and, because of the lack of moonlight, began to count. Dropped from a height of 500 feet he had been told that he would touch the ground when he reached twenty; instead his head hit it with a bang at thirteen and he was knocked unconscious for two or three minutes. He was still dizzy and shaken when he unfastened his parachute; getting up with difficulty, he found that he had sprained his left ankle.

His discomfiture was increased when the aircraft made its second run overhead and he had to dodge its dropped containers as they came hurtling down. He was helped to cover by the Air Operations Officer Evêque, whom he had already met in London. Trieur had landed safe and sound in the next field. Fortunately, the farmhouse where they were to spend the night was only half a mile distant, and Yeo-Thomas was able to hobble there painfully.

Next morning, although his ankle was still swollen, he determined to leave for Paris that afternoon: not until he was there could he get in touch with Abeille and Archer, who were in charge of the Brittany region, and with whom he hoped to be able to arrange a means of helping Bollaert and Brossolette. The farmer drove him and Trieur over rutty tracks covered with ice and put them in a bus which took them at a breakneck speed over even more slippery roads to Clermont-Ferrand. There they met and dined with Alain Bernay, the Regional Military Officer. Because of his hurry to get to Paris Yeo-Thomas refused Bernay's in-vitation to remain with him for a few days and visit the local groups, and Trieur and he caught the 11.30 train to the capital.

It is a favourite device of unoriginal film producers to translate to the chant of revolving railway train wheels the not particularly profound problems of their puppets: 'CAN I BE A BUSINESS GAL AND STILL BE A GOOD WIFE TO AL?' By the rules of such facile onomatopoeia Tommy ought to have heard the train wheels singing: 'BROSSOLETTE, BROSSOLETTE, BROSSOLETTE'. He heard nothing of the sort, nor did he require to: indeed, he sought relief from thinking about Brossolette in tipping off to the as yet un-tried Trieur some of the dodges which the saboteur would have to employ if he were to remain for long undetected in Paris.

As soon as he arrived in Paris he handed Trieur over to Maud,[2] who passed the saboteur on to Jacqueline Devaux,[3] who found him a flat. From Maud Tommy learned that Bollaert and Brossolette were still in Rennes prison, and that the latter was still believed to be a M. Pierre Boutet. Maud had established contact with some of the German of-ficials and, by bribing the guards and passing herself off to them as Boutet's mistress, had managed to send him food, wine and clothing in which were hidden messages to which Boutet had replied when sending out his linen to the laundry; by this means she had ascertained that Bollaert and Brossolette were relatively unmolested and that the latter's lock of white hair[4] had not yet begun to show.

His first night in Paris Tommy spent with the Peyronnets[5] whose flat in the Avenue des Ternes was again considered to be comparatively safe.

The next day while waiting to contact Abeille and Archer, he got in touch, through the ever faithful José Dupuis[6] with Pichard[7] and with Clouet des Pesruches, who, under the slightly less Boulevard-St Germain pseudonym of Galilée, was Air Operations Officer for the Touraine. From them he was able to obtain a clear idea of the situation in the Paris, Seine et Marne, Tours and western France areas. Partly because the recently stepped up parachutings had not yet been going on long enough for their impact to be felt throughout the country, the morale of Resistance was low. There were four main reasons for this: the weariness of constantly waiting and constantly disappointed reception committees; lack of arms; a growing belief that the Allies had no real intention of ever invading the Continent; and the increased vigilance of the Gestapo, now aided more and more by Darnand's Militia and the Lafont Organisation. It was the old story, with a few new drop scenes, and Tommy told his new version of the other old story to contradict it: parachuting operations were being formidably increased; Jérôme[8] was now in London demonstrating the great potentiality of the Maquis; and the invasion *would* take place.

Not wishing too greatly to inconvenience the Peyronnets, whose flat had already been watched by the Gestapo, Tommy spent his second night in Paris in Jeanne Helbling's[9] flat in the rue Casimir Pinel in Neuilly. Through his hostess he was able to contact Abeille and Archer. Abeille, who before the war had been a Prefect, immediately placed the whole of the Brittany organisation at Tommy's disposal for the rescue of Bollaert and Brossolette. But before determining upon a given course of action Yeo-Thomas decided to go to Rennes and conduct a preliminary investigation on the spot.

He left for Rennes on 1 March, taking Maud with him. With a local lawyer, who was a member of the Resistance, he discussed the possibility of getting Brossolette transferred on a trumped-up charge from Rennes prison to another prison in the south of France where he would be forgotten about by the Rennes authorities and whence they could ultimately secure his release on the basis of wrongful arrest. In the end they abandoned this plan which failed to take into account Bollaert and which would be a lengthy process involving the suborning of at least two Gestapo officers and the manufacture of an imaginary but convincing misdeed. Because of the danger of Boutet's real identity being discovered time was the essence of the problem which could, therefore, be solved only by force.

He then went to reconnoitre the prison and its precincts. Almost opposite the main entrance, there was a grocer's shop, whose owner was a member of one of the Resistance groups and who numbered among his customers most of the French and some of the German prison officials. From the grocer Yeo-Thomas learned that the greater part of the prison had been handed over to the Germans and only a few cells left free for the French; the main entrance was heavily guarded; all the gates were closed and at each gate was posted a sentry with a light machine gun which could be trained on every avenue of approach; a direct telephone line connected the guard room of the prison with that of an SS barracks not more than 600 yards distant. Tommy made a careful reconnaissance, found where the telephone line ran and where it could most easily be cut.

He saw at once that a frontal attack would be foredoomed to failure, but he soon hit upon a plan which he thought would stand a chance of success. When the telephone wire connecting the two guard rooms had been cut ten men from the local Resistance groups would keep watch from points of vantage situated in houses opposite the prison and would cover all approaches to the main gate. Three other men, of whom one would speak German perfectly and the other two fluently, would present themselves in German uniform with Sicherheitsdienst badges to the sentry at the main entrance; to him they would show forged instructions, supposedly emanating from the Paris or the Rennes Gestapo Headquarters and ordering the prison authorities to free Bollaert and Brossolette for transfer. Once in the guard room, where it was the custom for those in charge to verify such documents by telephoning to the Headquarters from which they purported to have been issued, the three disguised men would overpower the guards who, when not on sentry duty, so the grocer had said, always removed their belts and hung their weapons on the wall. The man who spoke perfect German would then return to the sentry at the main entrance, tell him that all was in order and ask him to open the gate so that a car, which would be waiting outside, could be brought into the yard in order that the prisoners might be picked up without attracting the attention of passers-by; the driver would back in and stop the car in such a position as to prevent the sentry from closing the gates again. Meanwhile the two other men would proceed into the prison proper, taking with them the corporal of the guard whom they would threaten to shoot immediately if he did not obey their orders. Bollaert and Brossolette would be brought out of their cells, put in the car and driven to a second car which would be waiting round the corner from the grocer's shop. While the second car took them to a safe hiding place in the centre of the town, the first car would continue south leaving an obvious trail behind it.

The plan seemed a good one, but it could not be put into action immediately: three German-speaking Resistance members, two cars and petrol had to be found; and, owing to a recent lack of parachuting operations in Brittany, Sten guns, pistols, hand grenades and ammunition would have to be brought to Rennes from a remote region.

Full of energy and confidence Yeo-Thomas returned to Paris and put the preparations in train. In the meantime he carried on with his official work: he held conferences with Sapeur and Commandant Palaud who were responsible for the paramilitary organisation of Paris, with 'Z' and with the leaders of Front National, Franc-Tireurs et Partisans, Ceux de la Libération, Ceux de la Résistance, and Organisation Civile et Militaire. Because of the repeated hold-ups by German police in the métro, and because vélo-taxis were rare, he had to do a great deal of walking: seven or eight contacts a day in places as widely separated as the Porte Maillot, the Boulevard St Michel, the Trocadéro, the Porte de St Cloud, the Parc Monceau and the Place de la Nation laid a considerable strain on his as yet imperfectly healed left ankle. He had also to take the usual precautions against being followed and to make sure that his contacts were not being trailed when he met them. For the Gestapo was more than ever alert: Pichard and Clouet des Pesruches were being hotly chased and José Dupuis had become so blown that she had had to be sent into the country for a month's rest. In view of this constant danger Tommy kept changing residences; but wherever he passed the night there was also a radio and once a week a cryptic message came over the BBC to assure him that Barbara had not been a casualty in the little blitz to which London was then being subjected. He was staying in Suni Sandöe's[10] flat in the rue Claude Chahu when he was informed that all was now in readiness for the attempt to rescue Bollaert and Brossolette from Rennes prison. Deciding to go to Rennes on the night of 21 March, and anxious to assure himself before he left that the air operations in the Touraine were running satisfactorily, he made an appointment for that morning with Antonin, a new agent-de-liaison lent to him by Pichard; Antonin was to bring him any messages he might have received from a girl called Brigitte who was Clouet des Pesruches' go-between, and to be prepared to pass on to Brigitte any instructions which Yeo-Thomas had for Clouet des Pesruches. The appointment had been fixed for 11 a.m. at the Passy métro station, situated, unlike most others, on a bridge above ground; Antonin was to walk down the steps on the left and Tommy was to come up them on the right: then start to cross in front of the newspaper kiosk next to the ticket office and to feign surprise when they met.

At 11 a.m. precisely Yeo-Thomas passed the kiosk, but Antonin was not there. Ordinarily Yeo-Thomas would not have broken his security rule of never waiting for an unpunctual contact, but it was imperative that instructions should be passed to Clouet des Pesruches at once in case he was detained in Rennes longer than he anticipated. He therefore went down the steps on the other side of the station and came up again, using the same steps as before. Having ascended the first flight and still seeing no sign of Antonin coming towards him he hesitated as to whether to pay a surprise visit to his father, whose flat was only 100 yards distant. Deciding to put duty before pleasure, he continued up the steps, meeting a crowd of people coming down from the train which had just arrived and feeling fairly safe in the other crowd which was climbing the steps towards the station. As he drew level with the last flight leading up to the ticket office five men in civilian clothes pounced on him, handcuffed him and began scientifically to search his pockets. Just then Antonin, escorted by another two Gestapo men in civilian clothes, passed by on the other side of the steps, looked at Tommy and was led away.

'*Wir haben Shelley*,' [We've got Shelley,] Tommy's captors shouted with glee.

The arrest of Yeo-Thomas was shortly before Brossolette was taken from Rennes for interrogation in Paris. He was either pushed or jumped from a window in Gestapo headquarters and died from his injuries, still refusing to reveal anything.

For Yeo-Thomas there began fourteen months of brutal persecution borne with unsurpassed courage and utter refusal to yield to his tormentors. During the Gestapo interrogation in Paris he was manacled, beaten, kicked and punched, held under water and then revived for further immersions, deprived of food and drink, and given no treatment for his injuries. This preliminary torture lasted without cease for forty-eight hours. Time and time again he merely quoted his name (Squadron Leader Kenneth Dodkin, his arranged identity), rank, and number.

He was then transferred to Fresnes prison, with a daily return to Gestapo headquarters for more questions under torture. In July, with the Allied armies advancing towards Paris, he was taken to a prison camp at Compiègne and then to Buchenwald, packed with 80 000 prisoners, the crematorium furnaces burning day and night to make room for the steady stream of new arrivals. With winter, some of the SS guards clearly became nervous about their ultimate fate with the realisation that Germany faced inevitable defeat.

Yeo-Thomas and a few other prisoners exploited this

reaction and staved off extermination by arranging to take the place of typhus victims who died in the notorious medical experiments block. With injections to produce violent fever Yeo-Thomas, now purporting to be a Frenchman, Maurice Chouquet, evaded the execution squads long enough to join a prisoners' convoy, evacuated from an area in danger of liberation, to the remote camp of Gleina, adjacent to a Jewish extermination camp. There Yeo-Thomas was put to work carrying corpses. In April this camp was also evacuated, a long line of sick and starving prisoners driven towards Chemnitz. They died at the rate of 170 every night. The chaos gave Yeo-Thomas the chance he had been waiting for, and he escaped, staggering on and on until he met some American troops.

Appropriately he managed to reach Paris on VE Day, 8 May 1945. He went to see his father, who had lived unmolested throughout the war. 'My son has returned,' he later told friends, 'but he looks like an old man of seventy.' Yeo-Thomas was then forty-four.

In February 1946, Wing Commander Yeo-Thomas, MC, was awarded the George Cross.

Notes

1 Colonel Passy, head of General de Gaulle's Bureau Central de Renseignements et d'Action, based in London. His real name was André Dewarrin. By the end of the war he held the DSO and MC as well as French and Norwegian decorations.
2 The cover name of Nicole Bauer, a cyclist messenger for the Resistance.
3 She provided a safe hide-out and meeting place.
4 Brossolette's distinctive lock of white hair on his black locks was known to the Gestapo. He dyed it black to conceal his real identity.
5 M. and Mme Peyronnet were relatives of Brossolette. Their sixteen-year-old daughter was a messenger for the resistance.
6 A school teacher, and friend of Yeo-Thomas.
7 An agent specialising in air operations sent from London.
8 The cover name of the leader of military groups of the Resistance throughout provincial France.
9 A French film actress who provided her luxury flat as a 'safe house' and message centre.
10 A Danish physical culture teacher working with the Resistance.

THE CHINDITS AT BLACKPOOL, BURMA

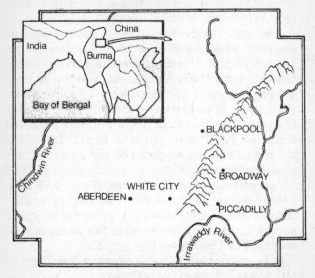

The war against the Japanese in Burma, who began to invade the country in January, 1942, was the most prolonged and exhausting British campaign in the Second World War. For the British and their American and Chinese allies the primary objects were to deal with the enemy across the border in China and to prevent the invasion of India.

An implacable enemy for friend and foe alike was Burma itself, a land of mountain ranges, wide rivers, vast areas of swamp and impenetrable jungle. For five months of the year tropical rains made great tracts impassable. In the hot season the blazing sun raised the temperature to 40°C (104°F). Malaria and other fevers were an ever-present menace, and the smallest wound or insect bite quickly festered.

Tanks, heavy guns, and armoured vehicles were

useless in most areas. Troops had to move on foot, clambering along mountain trails, hacking their way through dense jungle, wading in swamps, using mules as the only means of carrying arms and supplies. Beyond the few large towns the Japanese could do little more than maintain a network of outposts and strongpoints, manned by small companies of infantry.

To destroy them and to prepare for all-out war to drive the invader out of Burma Major General Orde Wingate planned a scheme he called Long Range Penetration. After hard training guerilla units were air-lifted, along with their mules, far behind enemy lines to attack Japanese outposts, destroy their food dumps, and cut communications.

This operation remained a secret until May, 1943, when one of the forces arrived back in India after three months of successful fighting. The men called themselves Chindits, a name derived from the Burmese word for the mythical animal which protected their temples from evil spirits.

General Wingate tragically died in an air crash in March 1944. But by then his daring plan was in full operation, involving the flying in of about 10 000 men and 1000 mules. Supplied and reinforced by RAF and US Army Air Force aircraft, Chindits built air strips, organised defences, and dealt with any of the enemy they could find. These outposts were given code names reminiscent of home – Aberdeen, Broadway, Piccadilly, White City, Blackpool. The last, the most northerly of them, is the scene of this story, told by the cipher officer who was there, on the staff of the 111 Indian Brigade, manned by Gurkhas with British officers.

Plans were cleared up and troops allocated. There was a general preparation for the task ahead. The column of Gurkhas was to remain behind at Mokso to provide a safe base for us in case we had to retreat. 'The trouble with —— Brigade', said Jack Masters,[1] 'was that they didn't have a foot on the ground.' This 'foot on the ground' was a bit of an obsession with our commander, but also a very wise precaution. I suppose that in Long Range Penetration the tendency is to thrust ahead in lightning raids with an emphasis on speed and mobility. This may easily result, and in some cases did, in a disregard of security, so that the striking force on meeting difficulty and suffering casualties had no safe base at which to reform. 'You must have a foot on the ground,' said Jack Masters. 'Unless you do you are like a boxer trying to hit out with one foot in the air. The result is that you lose your balance and are at the mercy of your opponent.' The column of the 3/4 Gurkhas was allotted the role of 'firm base' and ordered to remain at Mokso Sakan.

The Gurkha officers took rather a dim view of this plan, as they were denied the opportunity of a scrap. Mike Dibben, the column commander, accepted it all in his blasé, rather matter of fact manner. He never seemed to care about anybody or anything, a good companion but a very frank one. Mike McGillicuddy (of the Reeks), their transport officer, must have felt a bit sore. A member of the Irish gentry, impetuous and quite indefatigable, he used to charge up and down with a riding crop inspecting each mule and horse for badly placed loads or leg injuries. He was the officer who had distinguished himself so much in the scrap near Pinlebu.

With the Gurkhas stayed the majority of the brigade animals, another very wise precaution. In the 77 Brigade block at Mawlu dozens of mules had been killed by shellfire, as it was impossible to dig them in. They stood there patiently in the open and fell one by one. Frank Turner[2] remained behind with the animals and at last had a chance to look them over and rest them, feeling their backs and bellies and giving them a thorough grooming. Frankie Baines[3] also stayed behind with one of his defence platoons. He was very annoyed at this and said so emphatically, until Jack Masters had to ask him to desist. Poor Frankie. He was longing for his opportunity to fight and make good.

Perhaps later he was not so very sorry at what he had missed.

We marched over the pass. Frankie went on ahead with his platoon to guard the pass until we were through. We heard noises of firing and wondered if we would have a safe passage over the top. The track had been patched up in preparation for our march, but it was still in very bad condition and some recent rain had turned the dust into putty. At the top of the first rise we had a wonderful view of the Indawgyi Lake lying in a huge cluster of mountains, stretching north and south in a great green gash. The climb up was a series of small hills, up and down until we wondered exactly how much height we had gained. With every hill came a vista and the sight of the next climb. The pass came into sight suddenly round a corner and we were in a clearing with a few scattered *bashas* perched on the high ground with a magnificent prospect. There was a delightful cool air and we sat down to cool off. Frankie was roaring about after suspected Japs and disappeared south along the ridge; there was sound of much firing and news came of a fierce little engagement.

Confident that we would reach the valley by nightfall we struck along the ridge and then down through thick jungle, which grew steadily thicker. There had been some argument about the track we were following, and for good reason. The track became less and less distinct until we found ourselves confronted with almost impenetrable jungle. There was nothing to do but to slash through it with kukris, which slowed us down to a crawl. A night harbour in a thicket and an anxious glance at our schedule. Next day after some more furious hacking we reached the Namkwin Chaung and a delightful bivouac. We bathed and Doc Whyte[4] whistled, 'Moonlight becomes you.' 'Why are you so incurably optimistic, Doc?' I asked him. 'Well,' he replied, 'we must keep our spirits up.' John Hedley[5] was still very tired, but was trying to persuade himself that he was not, washing in the stream with tremendous vigour and his gurgling laugh. Jack Masters had informed Base that owing to the delay the block could not be put into position until 7 May, the following day. Chesty Jennings[6] was to go forward dressed as a Kachin and reconnoitre a site for a Dakota strip, as this had to be done in the open in broad daylight a mile from the main Jap lines of communication. I think that Jack Masters with that inventive mind of his was rather proud of this little ruse. He himself was to go forward and recce the block position.

7 May. Faltering progress down the Namkwin Chaung towards the valley, stops and starts and a lot of rude words. Briggo[7] set up a wireless on the steep bank of the *chuang* and cursed it into life with Jack Masters hovering round with a message and an itching pencil. Finally arrangements were made with Base; a supply drop on the day we moved into position; picks, shovels and wire. 'Essential dig in immediately. Maximum picks, shovels, wire required.' A lot would depend on our ability to prepare our position quickly. 77 Brigade had had a nasty scrap when half dug in and we were not keen to repeat the experience. Wire, wire and more wire. We must fence ourselves in and impale the enemy, shooting them as they struggled to break through. These were not pleasant thoughts, but we thought them. The General signalled urgently. The Dakota strip must be prepared with the minimum delay to fly in heavy weapons. Those first few days would be a gamble, and we knew it. A large force of enemy, and we were finished. Bad weather and no Dakota sorties, and we would have to clear out. We were working to a fine and rather anxious schedule.

Jack Masters went forward to make his recce, accompanied by Chesty in full Burmese garb. We sat down on the damp pebbles of the *chuang* and waited. There was an explosion somewhere in front. The pin had dropped out of an officer's grenade and there were several wounded men. We continued to sit, rather vague as to what was going on. Rations were opened and eaten cold; no fires. Dead minds and rather weary bodies; patience transformed into a sort of mental vacuum. Late in the afternoon our commander returned and we started on our way, off the *chuang* and up into a maze of ridges and sudden steep paths. It was further than we thought. Night fell and there was some confusion. I passed some troops already in position and hastily dug in by a little stream. Then up a steep, muddy path. Jack Masters in the darkness making frantic signals and asking the mortars where the ——— they thought they were going. I do not think they really knew. Left, up the final pull on to the ridge, steep as a cliff. Orders to dig in immediately. Briggo cursed, said he would do no such thing and lay down under a bush. I followed suit after a few scratches at the surface and found it difficult to prevent myself falling down the hill. On the flat ground to the east parachutes were falling. Picks, shovels, wire. Everything had worked out very well. Parties went off into the darkness to collect the loads while I lay back and felt a vague sympathy for everyone. I had only a slight idea where I was, but there were no Japs around, yet. The last Dakota droned away into the distance and there was silence, punctuated by the tramp of feet and the clink of picks and shovels.

As dawn came we could look round and take note. The position lay on a series of ridge features jutting out from the lower slopes of the hills we had just crossed. They were small ridges, but very sharp; what might, I suppose, be described as razor-edged. Brigade headquarters was sited in the middle at the top of the highest feature. Command Post on the east facing the valley, Signals and Intelligence on the west and the Dressing Station a little way down the path. To the west the position eased down into a small valley by a stream, facing the slopes of the mountains in all directions. This the King's Own defended through some very desperate days along the ridge that ran north-west by this little valley. East were two prong ridges thrust out into the valley held by the Cameronians. Below that was the valley, or rather The Valley, it was our target, the reason for all the battles of the next two weeks. Now it looked peaceful enough. A long narrow stretch of open country directly below, a river, and the railway a mile away. Namkwin village, with its little railway station, a prime target. The road, disappearing north to Mogaung and south to Indaw. On the far side of the valley were more hills and in these hills 77 Brigade was resting after its weeks of fighting at Mawlu; 14 Brigade was away to the south moving up from Banmauk to protect us and moving, as we thought, very slowly.

It was strange to sit down after all our wanderings without the thoughts of an early rise and march. Packs were flung down and we felt free men. We were no longer furtive. We were blatant, daring the Japs to come and crack us. We could look for the first time across open country and feel the open sky above us. We could light fires at any time instead of that brief hour in the evening, and we could walk about easily without the perpetual anxiety of the long, winding column and the jungle closing in on us. We knew what we were about and the issue was much clearer than in the hide-and-seek of yesterday. The valley lay below as a constant reminder of our task. Road and railway, block, no supplies north, Japs fall back, Stilwell advances south, we hand over and clear out. The sequence was logical and obvious to the simplest soldier. Rations, we were told, would be something better than K, which for all its ingenuity still left an aching void and an increasing distaste. The heat could be endured in a foxhole as it never could on the march.

But there was work. Dig and wire, dig and wire. Picks, shovels. More supply drops. Hauling the loads up the steep path. Mortars dug in uncomfortably near the headquarters. Jack Masters named the positions as on the cricket field — 'Wicket', 'Point', 'The Deep'. He drew diagrams, fire plans, expounded to commanding officers. Briggo demanded miles of wire and laid lines to every small outpost, wondering whether to lay them on the ground or above the undergrowth. The scene was peaceful enough, but we had a feeling that our days were numbered; there would be a time when little yellow men would be scrambling to get a footing on those slopes. If only we could dig in in time and face them with a jungle fortress instead of a few mud holes. Briggo and I marked out a site and got some Gurkha orderlies to dig. It was a palatial little place with ample

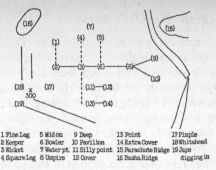

1 Fine Leg	5 Mid on	9 Deep	13 Point	17 Pimple
2 Keeper	6 Bowler	10 Pavilion	14 Extra Cover	18 Whitehead
3 Wicket	7 Water pt.	11 Silly point	15 Parachute Ridge	19 Japs
4 Square Leg	8 Umpire	12 Cover	16 Basha Ridge	digging in

Blackpool – dispositions of troops labelled in cricketing terms, from the official report to HQ from John Masters.

room and a solid roof of mud and timber but not much protection from artillery. The cipher office my NCOs constructed was an even flimsier device and would not have withstood a shell within twenty yards; the nearest was about twenty-five. We opened our packs and laid our equipment in neat rows along the shelf of the dug-out: tins, packets, ammunition, notebooks, water bottles and a large tin of adhesive plaster that I always carried around. It was all very good and we were going to enjoy ourselves.

Next night there was a burst of fire from the northern edge. We had not heard fire for a long time and raking through the night it was uncomfortable. Long, sustained bursts of Vickers and answering fire, the peculiar whippy cracks of Jap rifles. The firing continued for some time and it sounded like a big scrap. Maybe it was a company attack or a recce in force. Jack Masters phoned up the position, which was having no difficulty. There were lots of Japs, but mostly dead ones. They were wild and without a plan. Next morning we heard the full report and did not feel terribly pleased with ourselves. The attack had been launched by one platoon which had suffered many casualties, but the man on the Vickers had fired enough rounds to kill a battalion. It was an attack of jitters, an uneasy finger on the trigger, long bursts into the bushes which were moving. Perhaps we were not in for such a good time after all. The column was desperately tiring and monotonous, but perhaps weariness was better than fear. There was no sudden fire in the night and anxious inquiries on the telephone. There was only sleep, deep and unrestrained, against the rigours of the morrow. Here we could sleep all day, if we were not hauling loads or digging positions or doing guard or watering mules. But with the night came fear and our sleep would be broken by noise, and we would sit up in our foxholes waiting for the next burst, to place the fire, and then turn over in an attempt to knit up our fears in sleep. That first night brought us a foretaste of the future.

Our most urgent task after the initial defences was the construction of a glider strip. The gliders would bring in bulldozers and graders for a Dakota strip, the Dakotas would bring in guns and troops. It was all so easy, but we must hurry. It was a race with the Japs, who were well aware of our presence. The General sent messages continuously on the need for speed. He was worrying about the guns the Japs would bring up and realised our comparative helplessness against them as we stood. If we were to block the railway from our present position, only guns would do it. Chesty took gangs down the hill and dug and scraped in the paddy. Working at night they dodged parachutes, and by day they worked in full view of the Japs without any protection. Why did the Japs not attack them? But the Japs despite their habits were at times quite unpredictable. Perhaps they had received no orders.

Five hundred yards were cleared, leaving a good approach from the north, and a message was sent off to Base who replied that four gliders would arrive that night. But no gliders came; it was the weather. Next night we waited again. A message came at midnight saying that the sorties would be postponed until 0600 hours next day. At 0600 hours there was nothing, but about an hour later in broad daylight the first glider appeared, flying north up the valley at 500 feet. The tug circled, taking a good look at the strip, while below, the Japs opened up with light anti-aircraft fire. Then the glider was released north. The Jap machine-guns were now firing continuously. The glider came down until it was about 100 yards from the boundary, and then suddenly it banked round vertically when about fifty feet off the ground and plunged straight in with a great shudder and a crack which echoed up the valley. I was watching from the top of the hill and stood bewildered. One by one the gliders came in and one by one they crashed, until we had four wrecks on the paddy. Why, in broad daylight and with a perfect approach? I swore that gliders were doomed. Of the four pilots, two were killed and the remaining two, badly cut about the face, walked up to brigade headquarters. They said they could not see the strip distinctly. One of them said he must go back immediately and fly in another glider with the machinery. He did, a very brave effort. For the moment we were left with a bulldozer and a smashed grader. We could not build the strip until we had a new grader, and until we built the strip we could get no heavy weapons. If the Japs caught us now we would have little to say for ourselves.

Next morning came the shells. I was woken up at about 5.30 by a whistle and a bang. But they were far away and did not concern us. I turned over and dozed. But the bangs continued nearer, until fear could not be kept back. We were in range and we were being destroyed. A distant thud, then we would get lower in our foxholes, a whine and then a deathly pause. Explosion, a shower of trees and mud. Silence. Then again the distant thud. There was no escaping this. It was steady and relentless. John Hedley sat in his trench counting the shells, their bearing and estimated calibre. He was lucky to have something to engage him. My NCOs sat in their flimsy shelter enciphering messages, working with awkward breaks and pauses and a great inward tension. Jock Yuille[8] cracked jokes and raised a few nervous laughs.

We knew fear that morning in a new way. We had no guns to answer back, our planes would have great difficulty in spotting them. We would be destroyed. 'There will be no retreat from the Block,' said Wingate. Instead of retreat were we to sit here and be consumed?

At last the noise ceased and men crept from their holes. Briggo learnt from Jack Masters that there were plenty of bodies about. When one of my NCOs later reported for duty, he was white and shaking like a leaf. He had just been digging out his pals who lay buried round him. A message was sent to Base reporting 300 shells and moderate casualties: twenty-four killed, twenty wounded. The General replied, 'Well done.' 'Why well done?' asked my gloomy sergeant, who always knew far too much about what was going on. 'The sooner we get a few guns the better.' I think many of us prayed for guns, and though the day was peaceful we felt very ill at ease.

Work on the Dakota strip continued all day and into the night. The scraper was working intermittently and progress was very slow. Still the Japs did not intervene, but continued to watch the troops as they scraped at the paddy. The American engineers were in charge and Chesty stood by. The scene was a very peaceful one and the chug of the bulldozer sounded like the noise of a tractor and binder in an English summer. It was summer all right, but just over there were the Japs. There was a difficulty over the strip; a large bump at the north end which was the approach end. A second day, and all day they scraped at that bump. The General was getting anxious, but no more so than us. At last the strip was considered fit to take Dakotas and the codeword 'Texas' was flashed to Base.

The first Dakota was overhead when it was discovered that the strip was only 750 yards long and not the required 1200. The pilot was told and asked if he wanted to have a try. He switched on his landing lights and came up to the boundary. There was a bump as he pulled back too soon, a bounce and then with full throttle he was off again – he landed in India on his belly. The second one, carrying some engineer equipment, approached next, dropped over the hedge and pulled up. Magnificent. The plane was unloaded and roared off again into the night. No one else tried their luck. Jack Masters sent a message to Base, 'Regret Texas muddle due error estimation, co-ordination.'

Next day we scraped and levelled, and reported that although there was still a big bump the strip was the required length and had a perfect approach. 'Texas' was signalled again and the flare path lit. The planes came in one by one and I watched from the hill. There was always a moment of agony as they throttled down, whether they had come too low, too high, too fast. One plane burst a tyre, shot off into the paddy and burst into flames. A gunner major standing next to me turned away, saying 'I hope to goodness none of my men were in that.' He was dead twenty-four hours later. The crew got out of the blazing plane – there were no passengers – and walked off; Chesty dived gallantly into the plane to rescue the mail. I walked down the strip to collect personnel. It was an amazing scene, a continuous roar of engines, huge flashing lights and an organised chaos of men deplaning, stores being offloaded and jeeps rushing about with trailers behind them. These jeeps were the first wheeled vehicles we had seen. Our column RAF officers were controlling and with every pilot wanting to get down and get off it was not an easy task. A plane came careering madly down the runway and we ran for it. After some very irregular manoeuvres it came to rest facing across the strip. The American pilot leaned out of the cockpit and shouted, 'Gee, I guess I must have had my fingers crossed.' A jeep hauled him round again and he was soon off. As each pilot got out he would look at the blazing plane and ask nervously, 'Who is that?' A damaged Dakota, which would not be repaired, stood by the side of the strip. A Yank approached me and said, 'Is that going free? I'd like the radio. I'm kinda mad on radio.' I assured him it was going and he climbed in complete with screwdriver, followed by a lot of other Americans. I followed them in and seeing that the clock had gone took the first-aid kit.

Then Luke[9] came up out of the darkness. He had left us just before we flew into Burma and was now on Dakotas. 'Hello, I didn't recognise you, R. J. How are the others?' Very well, I said, and how did he like our strip? A bit of a bump at one end. 'Bump!' he shouted, 'it's a mount'n. We were doing 100 on the clock when I last looked and let her down nicely. Then wow! up we went. Pretty rugged. Well, so long.' He strode off.

The two gliders bringing the chassis and body of a scout car were overhead. All Dakotas were given red and we waited anxiously. They cast off, then up north. A steep bank and a perfect touchdown. Whew! The glider was pushed off the strip and we looked for the other one. The crew of the first glider could hardly bear to look, and we realised at once the terrific tension these pilots had to face. 'He's gone too far away,' he yelled and turned his back. But he was wrong. The glider came in very nicely; it did not attempt to brace until it was almost on top of a Dakota when it pulled up sharply. Two complete gliders, a record. A British soldier rushed up to the glider pilot and asked him if he would swop uniforms.

There was another pile-up. An RAF plane came in very fast and showed no inclination to slow up. It careered past the dispersal bay and piled up on the paddy. Some rather bewildered and shaken REME personnel scrambled out followed by the crew who thought it was all rather a joke. We were just preparing to unload it when there was a bang and a whistle of bullets. I did not realise immediately what had happened until I saw the others run madly across the strip. I followed them and thought that if there was a more naked place than an airstrip I would like to hear of it. We crouched behind the bales of supply containers feeling rather foolish. An officer exhorted us gallantly to charge the enemy. But I swore that if ever I did that I must first know where the enemy was. The last Dakota roared off down the strip, did a ground loop and hobbled slowly back. The men were now dead tired and dawn was breaking. I went up to Jack Masters to explain the situation and to ask for relief to be sent down. This he did promptly. When day broke the loads were still being hauled up the hill.

We had guns. We were able to answer back to that early morning horror: 25-pounders; Oerlikons; Bofors. As they were hauled up the steep path men gathered round and cheered. We were helpless no longer.

But there was work, continuous wearing work hauling ammunition and supplies up the long track. And then the enemy came. He came in at 'The Deep' and he came with a set purpose. There were not platoons this time, but companies. A continuous roar through the night and anxious voices over the telephone. During the day we would call up planes and Cochran's force (we called them the Young Ladies[10] – older readers will recognise the nickname) would treat us to some fun. Mustangs dived down the narrow valley which separated us from the enemy, firing a few yards from the noses of our troops. Then came the Mitchells with their parachute bombs, which on the first occasion gave us a bit of a surprise. The Japs were given no respite except at night, when they would emerge and renew their attack on the King's Own, rushing wildly at the wire and getting no further. We were holding and killing, but we were also tiring. The firing used to start at dusk. First the 105 mm, then the 75 mm, which gave us little chance to go to ground, the mortars, the grenades and finally the machine-guns. There was an expectancy with each dusk, waiting for the distant thud and the whine, the sharp bang and explosion of the 'whizz-bang', the more open crash of mortars and grenades. Men charged the wire and died as they tried to get over, men blown up on our mines or maimed by our booby traps. In headquarters we heard merely the noise and chatter of the weapons and could only wait for news. With the morning came relief but also an overriding weariness, fatigues on the airstrip, digging and guarding. The King's Own were being steadily worn down and they knew it.

Then one night the Japs decided to finish it all off. That dusk was a noisier dusk than usual and the shells were more persistent. As darkness fell the smaller weapons opened up and the Japs massed. Late at night came distressing news from 'The Deep'. A platoon had been heavily shelled and in its present state was not in a position to offer much resistance. The Japs might break through here, and if they broke through we would have little chance of ejecting them. Briggo went off to take some more ammunition to 'The Deep' and Jack Masters rang up the Cameronians telling them to bring up a platoon. Tim Brennan, their second-in-command, came hurrying up and they went into a huddle. Better stand by until the situation cleared a bit. Our commander rang up the King's Own. The platoon which had been so badly mauled had reorganised and was in a position to fight again; the casualties were less than had been at first feared. The fighting died away and the dawn came very beautiful.

The Japs beat a retreat. The constant hammering of the last few days, if it had tried us, had cruelly hurt the enemy. A patrol was sent out into the Jap position and found carnage and desolation; a blood-stained dressing-station and bloody equipment scattered about. There were no bodies of course — the Japs had taken care of that — but evidence enough of a mighty slaughter. We sent a message to Base giving the situation, not quite sure of the enemy's intentions but knowing that we had given him a nasty battering.

Gradually the position at Blackpool became untenable. The rains began, and in the rainy season supply dropping aircraft could not reliably operate to bring food and ammunition. Shelling by the encroaching enemy caused a steady stream of casualties. Infantry attacks began at night. In the morning the barbed wire defences were strewn with dead Japanese, hit by mortar and rifle fire. In the last week of May 1944, the Chindits withdrew, after beating off an enemy force of 2000 for a fortnight. They faced an appalling journey through jungle and over a mountain pass, helping their sick and wounded comrades, short of food, and wary of the ever-lurking Japanese snipers. They reached comparative safety — only to receive orders for more fighting.

But the Chindits like these men at Blackpool had paved the route to victory. During 1944 the 14th Army grew into the largest single British army of the Second World War, with a strength of a million men. They came from United Kingdom regiments, from India, and from East and West Africa. Emulating the Chindits' operations on a massive scale, entire divisions were moved, and their supplies maintained, by air. Later, almost incredible feats of engineering created hundreds of kilometres of roads surfaced with sacking soaked in bitumen; huge rafts powered by outboard motors ferried supplies along the rivers. The longest Bailey bridge in the world was thrown across the river Chindwin. Wrecked railways were repaired, and locomotives brought from India in pieces and assembled on the site.

The Japanese continued to attack fanatically, suffering terrible casualties. In one battle 65 000 dead, sick and wounded were left from a force of 115 000. Fighting went on and on against impossible odds, formal surrender for a Japanese soldier being out of the question. Only after the Emperor broadcast the cease-fire from Tokyo did the starving remnants of the Imperial Japanese forces in Burma tardily lay down their arms. For the 14th Army the long and bitter campaign ended in total victory, a triumphant success for a kind of fighting never previously known.

Notes

[1] Major Jack Masters, later Lieutenant Colonel and Commander of 111 Brigade.

[2] Major Frank Turner, in charge of the Gurkha mule leaders.

[3] Baines was a colourful character, officially an expert on camouflage, originally attached to the group in India. He was smuggled into Burma.

[4] Captain Desmond Whyte, medical officer.

[5] Major John Hedley was Brigade Intelligence Officer.

[6] Squadron Leader R. J. Jennings, expert on the air operations supporting the group. He was nicknamed Chesty because of his massive physique.

[7] The signals officer.

[8] Corporal Yuille was the author's NCO.

[9] An officer in the United States Army Air Force.

[10] Colonel Philip Cochran, in charge of No. 1 Air Commando. The nickname for his force originated from a famous pre-war chorus line in London musical shows produced by C. B. Cochran and known as Cochran's Young Ladies.

THE RED DEVILS AT ARNHEM

After five years of the Second World War the Nazi armies were being relentlessly driven back to the original frontiers of the Reich. By early September 1944, Paris had been liberated and the US 1st and 3rd Armies were rolling towards the Franco-German border. The Canadian 1st Army was mopping up the remaining enemy pockets on the Channel coast and the British 2nd Army was poised to liberate Brussels. Far to the south the US 7th Army and the Free French 1st Army were moving towards the Upper Rhine after landing on the Riviera coast.

These enormous forces, stretching farther and farther from their starting points, presented formidable problems of supply. The Supreme Commander, General Eisenhower, had to organise food, fuel and arms for some $2\frac{1}{4}$ million men and nearly half a million vehicles, with no major ports on the Channel coast in Allied hands. The spectacular advance ground almost to a halt, faced by Germany's defences in depth, the *Westwall*, plus the natural barrier of the Rhine.

Field Marshal Montgomery proposed a solution. The *Westwall* could be by-passed at its northern end, this route not only allowing the port of Antwerp to be taken, but opening the way straight to Germany's industrial heart, the Ruhr. The breakthrough would be achieved by capturing the great road bridge over the Rhine in the Dutch town of Arnhem. To reach it meant crossing three wide canals and two rivers, the Maas and the Waal. The operation, code-named Market Garden, involved dropping an entire army corps from the air, with the British 1st Airborne Division, named by the enemy the Red Devils, under the command of Major General R. E. Urquhart, capturing the bridge of Arnhem, and the US 82nd and 101st Airborne Divisions taking the bridges over the canals and the two rivers. Simultaneously the British Guards Armoured Division and the XXX Corps would advance through Eindhoven for some 70 kilometres to join up with the airborne troops dropped at Arnhem. The day chosen for this imaginative and unique operation was 17 September 1944.

The initial landings, though delayed by autumn morning mists on British airfields, were successful, and by mid-afternoon the units were fighting their way towards the bridge, 13 kilometres from the dropping zone. But the number of crack German troops, including the 9th and 10th Panzer Divisions, and the strength of the defences, were much greater than intelligence sources had reported. Casualties during the first twenty-four hours were heavy. However, the landing zones for the second wave of men and material were intact, and the enemy's efforts to destroy those troops who had battered their way as far as the approaches to the bridge had been beaten off. Everything depended on the reinforcements to be dropped by mid-morning on the second day.

The morning of the 18th dawned bright and clear; the

second lift was due at 10.00 hours, and shortly before that hour Major Wilson[1] and his men laid out more markers to make sure that the landing and dropping zones would be recognised. They had been informed that any aircraft seen would be friendly; but as they were engaged on their work a number of Messerschmitt 109s dived upon them, guns blazing. They leapt for cover and fortunately escaped casualties. 10.00 hours came, then 11.00 hours, then noon, and still there was no sign of the Dakotas, the tugs and the gliders. These were still in England, for clear though the weather was over Holland, the low cloud and fog so prevalent during the summer and autumn of 1944 persisted over the airfields, and it was not possible to take off.

Eventually rain drove the mist away sufficiently to allow the second lift to take the air, and by 15.00 hours it was beginning to arrive at Arnhem. 'In addition to our American crew there were eighteen of us in my stick,' records Major R. T. H. Lonsdale, DSO, MC, second-in-command of the 11th Battalion, whose tenacity at Primosole[2] had been of such value, 'we were flying at 800 feet as we crossed the Suffolk coastline, and I remember looking down on the old town of Aldeburgh and its quiet streets and wishing myself there. One's thoughts get a bit mixed at times. Some of the fellows read, some of them talked. My batman – Lance-Corporal "Nobby" Noble – was, as usual in a plane, sound asleep. I glanced outside at the rest of the Dakotas. Well, I reflected, we've plenty of company, and we're all going the same way.

'We were still at 800 feet when we made the Dutch coast, and we kept over our own lines as long as possible. The first warning that we were approaching the dropping zone came from the co-pilot. "You've half an hour," he announced tersely. Ten minutes later the red light by the exit door signalled the "Get ready". We stood up and made a last check. There was nothing much to say.

'By now we had skirted Nijmegen and were over enemy-held territory. The luck was holding – we'd had no interference yet. Suddenly, it seemed right from beneath our feet, a crackling noise was instantly followed by a whip-like explosion. The plane lurched violently, flung us sprawling, then righted again. No need to ask if we'd been hit – we knew it. The air-burst – I reckon that was what it was – tore a great rent in the fuselage and wounded two of my lads in the leg. The American crew chief standing by the door was only partly saved by some armour-plating. I looked at my right hand and was surprised to see it streaming blood.

'We had barely time to unhook our casualties and move them to the back of the plane – "no jump today, boys" – when we got the green light to drop. The crew chief, although wounded, stuck to his post and saw us off. I was glad to go.

'I suppose we could not have been in the air more than thirteen seconds, but that was enough. The Jerry tracer came streaking among us; I never felt more like a sitting pigeon than I did then. Obviously the enemy had brought up their mobile flak units after the events of the previous day, and they gave it us hot.

'I touched down in the centre of a field, with the entire brigade dropping around. The Americans had dropped us slap in the right place, and I give them full marks for that. They didn't all get back. As I slipped out of my harness I watched one of their Dakotas crash in flames. Noble – good old "Nobby" – came dashing up to me. I'd bled a lot, and a stiffener from my flask helped me as he hurriedly bandaged my hand.'

The drops and the glider landings of the second lift were as successful as those of the day before. Once more the RAF and American crews had performed their task with skill. On this occasion one of them showed that type of resolution which makes a man faithful unto death. Over the dropping zone a Dakota with sixteen parachutists on board was hit and set on fire. 'Suddenly a little orange flame appeared on the port wing,' notes a witness. 'I watched the plane gradually lose height and counted the bodies baling out. They all came out, although the last two were too low for comfort. But the crew stayed in the plane and flew straight, the flames getting larger and larger till eventually it flew into the ground.'

The 4th Parachute Brigade were dropping through the air to 'the clack of bullets and the thump of mortars. There were fires burning all over the heath. Quite a wind was blowing, and many found themselves in the fir woods. The speed with which we dropped down out of the trees was fantastic, for we had heard stories about parachutists in trees in Normandy'.

Once on the ground, the individual battalions began to form up, and the 11th Battalion had collected some eighty prisoners before it reached the rendezvous. The 4th Parachute Brigade, under Hackett,[3] was composed of the 156th, 10th and 11th Battalions, who were soon ready to fulfil their appointed task. Hackett was in high fettle, for 'two of the enemy gave themselves up to me about two minutes after I was out of my parachute harness, and I had a couple of prisoners even before I had a command post'. He was met by Lieutenant Colonel C. B. Mackenzie, the GSO1 of the division, who described the situation. The fierceness of the opposition in Arnhem had caused Brigadier Hicks to change his plans. The 156th and 10th Battalions were to carry out their original orders, seize and hold the high ground north of Arnhem which had proved too difficult a task for the 1st Battalion; but the 11th Battalion was to make with all speed for the bridge, together with the other two companies of the 2nd Battalion of the South Staffordshire Regiment which had now arrived.

This force, the South Staffordshires in the van, lost no time in setting out. They moved but slowly, but by the time darkness fell had reached the western outskirts of Arnhem. Here they fell in with the harassed but indomitable Dobie,[4] whose 1st Battalion had already lost four-fifths of its strength. About 20.00 hours the three commanding officers, Dobie, McCardie[5] in command of the South Staffordshires, and Lea[6] of the 11th Battalion, held a conference not far from the Elizabeth Hospital. It was decided that the advance should begin again at 04.00 hours on the morning of Tuesday, the 19th, that was in about six hours. The 1st Battalion was to move down to the river bank, turn left and make their way towards the bridge, followed by the 11th Battalion. The South Staffordshires were to move down the main road.

At the chosen hour the South Staffordshires began to advance, only to be held up at a spot called the Monastery in the main street of Arnhem. Here they lost heavily, being overrun by tanks after their Piat ammunition had been exhausted. Withdrawing westwards, they reorganised and then delivered an attack on the Den Brink position which had proved so troublesome to the 1st Battalion when on its way to the bridge. The object was to make it possible for the 11th Battalion to reach a road running north from Den Brink. For a little time the gallant South Staffordshires prevailed, but hardly had they appeared on the high ground when enemy tanks drove them off it, and at the same time attacked the 11th Battalion, which was deprived of any chance it might have had to deliver the assault planned a few hours before. Taken in front and on a flank, the battalion suffered heavily, though the left-hand and rear companies were able to extricate themselves. The German tactics were those of men well trained: their tanks remained out of range of Piats, and 'solemnly knocked houses down or burnt them by firing phosphorus shells at the roofs, and then waited till the defenders were forced to withdraw or be burnt to death. German infantry, covered by the tanks, infiltrated between houses and gardens and mopped up the defenders or forced them back'.

Meanwhile the 156th Battalion, followed by the 10th, was moving along the line of a railway towards the high ground, its chosen objective. By nightfall on the 18th the first of these had reached the railway station at Wolfhezen, and the second was about a mile away. Hackett decided that at dawn on the next day the 156th Battalion should capture the village of Koepel to the north of Arnhem, while the 10th should form a firm base 1000 yards in front of the little village of Johanna Hoeve.

The 156th Battalion's attack began at 05.00, and by 10.00 hours had petered out after an initial success. By then its casualties were on a par with those sustained by the other battalions in this operation, and 'A' Company had lost all its officers. Nor was the 10th Battalion more fortunate: in moving to its assigned position it soon encountered the inevitable barrage of anti-aircraft guns used as light artillery, self-propelled guns and tanks. The battalion dug in with speed and address on either side of the Arnhem-Utrecht road, the intention of Lieutenant Colonel Smyth being to endure the enemy's fire while day lasted and then to deliver a night attack with the object of reaching the Hoeve position. Through the long day the Battalion stood its ground, though mortar fire was added to its other tribulations. The behaviour of Captain L. E. Queripel, during these heavy hours, was especially noteworthy. Commanding a company to which men separated from two other battalions had attached themselves, he crossed and re-crossed the road under heavy fire to encourage his men and put them in position. At one moment, finding a wounded sergeant, he picked him up and took him to the regimental aid post, receiving a wound in his face while doing so. His next feat was to lead a small local attack against a strongpoint composed of a captured British anti-tank gun and two machine-guns. He killed the crew of all three, and the anti-tank gun thus recovered proved of great service.

As the autumn day waned the 10th Battalion found itself unable to hold on any longer and began slowly to withdraw. Queripel, cut off with a small party of men, took cover in a ditch. In addition to the wound in his face, he had now been wounded in both arms. He and his men lined the ditch to cover the withdrawal of the remainder of the battalion. By then they were short both of weapons and ammunition, having but a few Mills bombs, rifles and their personal pistols. German infantry were very near and more than once their stick bombs landed in the ditch, only to be flung back in their faces by the vigilant Queripel. The position became more and more untenable, but he waited until the last moment before he ordered those of his men still alive to leave while he covered their withdrawl with the aid of such grenades as remained. 'That was the last occasion on which he was seen.' His gallantry earned him a posthumous Victoria Cross. Queripel's gallantry and the steady shooting of Sergeant Kincaid and Private Waters, both of the Intelligence section, who could claim among their victims the crew of a German self-propelled gun, enabled the battalion to dig in once more and to hold its position, though by now the enemy had brought up several tanks. 'These soon received a taste of the Piat and did not like it.'

Thus before 19 September was ended everything had gone awry. The utmost efforts of the 1st and 3rd Battalions, and later of the 11th, to cut their way through the town to the bridge, had failed; and the 156th and 10th Battalions, somewhat to the north, had been equally unfortunate. The day was marked by two further disasters. In the afternoon the first supplies from the air were flown in, but since the division had been unable to make any contact with Dempsey's 2nd Army, no message had been sent warning Nos. 38 and 46 Groups of the RAF that the supply dropping point chosen beforehand to the north of Warnsborn was a considerable distance from any ground held by the division. Despite the display 'of every kind of sign and indicator', the pilots flew through heavy anti-aircraft fire to deposit their loads on the agreed spot. They fell into the hands of the Germans, who, strangely enough, did not keep them for themselves, but issued them to the local Dutch population. Even had the pilots seen the desperate signals made to them – they do not appear to have done so – they would in all probability have regarded them as a *ruse de guerre* and ignored them.

Then the arrival of the gliders belonging to the Polish Parachute Brigade provoked the most violent reaction on the part of the enemy; much of it fell on the unhappy 4th Parachute Brigade, then endeavouring to conform to a new, and for Urquhart a most melancholy decision. By the afternoon of Tuesday, the 19th, he was forced to face the unpalatable fact that all attempts to reach the bridge by the reinforcements, whether parachute troops or glider-borne, had failed and would continue to fail; for the enemy was very strong, and, moreover, possessed armour and heavy weapons. Accordingly, with the utmost reluctance he decided that he must form a perimeter round the little suburb of Oosterbeek, in the midst of which were his headquarters at the Hartestein hotel, and there hold out until the 2nd Army, if it was coming, arrived. This decision meant that the bridge, to which Frost still clung, and of which the seizure had been the main objective of the operation, must be abandoned.

The necessary orders, issued with no little difficulty, were carried out that night and next day. In obeying them, further losses, inevitable with troops in close contact with the enemy seeking to disengage themselves, occurred. The 156th Battalion lost all but a quartermaster and six men of 'S' Company, half 'B' Company and all 'C' Company when moving to their places in the perimeter. And on the next day, the 20th, the 200 officers and men left fought a series of fierce actions in an attempt to cover the withdrawal of the 10th Battalion towards the perimeter. Their numbers dwindled steadily and not more than four officers and seventy other ranks survived to share in the last defence. The 10th Battalion, whom they had sought so hard to aid, suffered equally and was virtually wiped out. 'We were given orders,' reported Sergeant Bentley afterwards, 'to leave the wood. It was every man for himself, for by then we were all split up ... Sergeant Sunley and Sergeant Houghton were terrific. We ran across a playing field and found several men showing yellow triangles. We understood that they were Poles ... we had by then lost about two-thirds, but the men were still in good heart.'

During these efforts to move back to Wolfhezen and then to the perimeter one of its non-commissioned officers, Corporal Garibaldi, did not belie the famous name he bore. At a point where the woods receded he charged the enemy in his Bren-gun carrier and silenced their fire, only to be killed later. Eventually Lieutenant Colonel Smyth and Major Warne, the commanding officer and the second-in-command, with about sixty other ranks, were all that were left standing when the final position was reached.

The remnants of one other battalion belonging to the brigade, the 11th, also eventually took up a position in the perimeter. That battalion, it will be recalled, had been sent towards the bridge with the South Staffordshires in a last effort to reinforce Frost,[7] and had been almost entirely destroyed. A few men under Lieutenant J. E. Blackwood of 'B' Company succeeded in withdrawing in accordance with Urquhart's plan.

In this heavy fighting the brigadier and those with him took their full share. 'My brigade headquarters,' wrote Hackett months later when he had returned from Holland, 'with its clerks, signallers, intelligence section and batmen, was holding the centre of our line as a unit. They were a splendid lot. The signallers were mostly Cheshire yeomen . . . the clerks were also "foundation members" for the most part and in the close-quarter fighting in the woods on 19 and particularly 20 September did brilliantly under Staff Sergeant Pearson, the chief clerk, one of the bravest men at really hand-to-hand fighting and one of the soundest in the brigade. . . . I found myself on 20 September as "a broken-down cavalry-man" (Urquhart's phrase) leading little bayonet rushes in the very dirty stuff the brigade had to contend with before we made contact with the division, and I was impressed with the stout hearts and accurate grenade throwing of the brigade Intelligence section, particularly after the Intelligence officer (Captain Blundell) was shot and killed at about 20 yards range on the same morning.'

Thus did the remnants of the 4th Parachute Brigade make ready with the rest of Urquhart's force for the last round. To some extent the brigade's fortunes, or rather misfortunes, were even more remarkable than those of the 1st. Its three battalions, the 156th, 10th and the 11th, in their attempt to carry out the original plan and form the outer perimeter round Arnhem, had immediately to face a situation which made the fulfilment of their task impossible however hard they tried – and their efforts were heroic. The reason is not far to seek. They arrived in the neighbourhood of Arnhem, but, be it remembered, eight miles away from the town, on 18 September, and they formed the major part of the second lift. By then all chance of effecting surprise had vanished and they were at once face to face with an alert enemy determined to offer fierce resistance. 'We had gunshot casualties in the air,' records Hackett, 'and during the reorganisation period on the ground it was disconcerting to walk into scattered parties of Boches, usually pretty frightened, fortunately, for the most part lying close in the heath and sometimes only flushed when you nearly stepped on them.' Thus the brigade found itself committed to immediate battle almost before it had reached the ground. Moreover, the fighting from first to last was at close quarters and endured for eight days, of which the last four were spent manning a dwindling perimeter. In these circumstances it is possible, even probable, that the 4th Parachute Brigade's casualties in killed and wounded were even higher than those of the 1st. After the battle was over, so few remained that it was disbanded and never reformed.

Of the 1st Parachute Brigade in the perimeter there was no sign. Dobie, commanding the 1st Battalion, had received orders at 01.00 hours on Tuesday, the 19th, to withdraw to Oosterbeek, but these were later cancelled and he and his men moved in accordance with the plan concocted earlier to the river. Here they turned left-handed with a high bank rising steeply on their left, and here, meeting with German infantry, they fought with them hand to hand. Major Perrin-Brown led a bayonet charge of 'T' Company, and a little later Major Timothy, another of 'R' Company, and the morning air was filled with the battle cry of 'Waho Mahommed' springing from the throats of desperate but indomitable men. Soon after dawn the battalion was attacked by tanks, and by 06.00 hours 'our position was becoming desperate, as the enemy were on high ground and in houses above us, and tanks were firing at point-blank range'. The strength of the battalion at that moment was, 'R' Company, six men; 'S' Company, fifteen; 'T' Company, eight; battalion headquarters, ten. Dobie, making a personal reconnaisance, saw at once that any further move was out of the question. He ordered what was left of his command to enter the nearby houses. They were occupied by Germans, who flung grenades at them, one of which wounded him. With six men Dobie eventually forced an entry into a house and made for the cellars, which were full of civilians. Only two men of his party were unwounded. Here they remained for about an hour until some SS troopers entered and took them prisoner.

The 3rd Battalion was a little better case. Precisely how many officers and men belonging to it reached the perimeter is not known. After the final withdrawal, when a roll-call was called at Nijmegen, one officer and thirty-six other ranks answered to their names.

The 21st Independent Parachute Company under Wilson, and the Sappers under Captain H. F. Brown, played their full part. Wilson's men, among whom were a number of anti-Nazi Germans, were particularly fierce. Meeting with snipers belonging to an SS Battalion near the dropping zone before the second lift came in, they attacked them fiercely, and presently 'the Germans, in their snipers' suits, crawled out of their slit trenches and grovelled on the ground begging for mercy. They were terrified to see men in red berets and had to be violently persuaded to their feet'. Somewhat later in the battle the Germans shouted to them to surrender. 'We shouted back', says Wilson, 'that we were too frightened to do so, and that they must come and get us. Sixty of them were fools enough to do so, and were wiped out with twelve Bren guns at a range of 150 yards. They died screaming.'

The sappers fought as infantry with great effect.

Before recounting the last stand at Oosterbeek, what happened to Frost and the 2nd Battalion must first be recorded. That Monday night, the 18th, which began in flame and smoke from the burning houses, gradually grew quieter, until soon after midnight 'there was absolute silence, or so it seemed to me', said Frost, 'for some hours'. The commander of the defence was able at last to snatch some sleep. Up till then he had had but half an hour, and had sustained himself with cups of tea and an occasional nip of whisky. Before dawn he had had to issue an order bringing sniping to an end, for ammunition was running low and would have to be kept for warding off the attacks which the enemy was bound soon to launch with increasing severity. The bridge was still covered by the guns of the 1st Air Landing Light Regiment under Lieutenant Colonel W. F. K. Thompson, Royal Artillery, but these were their only support. 'It became more and more difficult to move,' recounts Frost, 'for the Boche were tightening their grip, though they made no effort to close with us. By then the number of wounded was very great, but the number of killed small.'

The men at the bridge held on throughout that day, buoyed up by rumours, first that the 1st and 3rd Battalions were at hand, and then in the later afternoon by the news that the South Staffordshires and the 11th Battalion were fighting their way towards them. It was a day of heavy mortaring and shelling by tanks which had crept up to a position close to the river bank. Towards noon Captain A. Franks went out against them, and scored three hits with the last three Piat bombs. The German tanks clattered away out of range and did not return. At dusk, however, a Tiger tank appeared and shelled in turn each house still held by the parachutists. Among the casualties caused by this fire was Father Egan, MC, who had served with the brigade from the outset, and Major A. D. Tatham-Warter. They were both hit, but both remained with those still fighting and refused to go below to the cellars.

During this day the conduct of Trooper Bolton of the 1st Air Landing Reconnaissance Squadron was particularly noteworthy for the calmness with which he manned his Bren gun and refused to be parted from it. 'He hated the thought of anyone using it but himself,' says Captain Ber-

nard Briggs, the staff captain at brigade headquarters, who
had been at the bridge from the beginning, 'and would wake
from a cat-nap at any moment and leap to it ready to fire'.
Lieutenant P. J. Barnett, of the brigade headquarters
defence platoon, showed much courage and ingenuity when
he succeeded in destroying 'a troublesome tank single
handed with grenades'. He was to earn the Medaille
Militaire Willemswoorde, the Dutch Victoria Cross.

Night fell and it seemed to Frost, looking uneasily over
his shoulder, that the whole town of Arnhem was on fire, including two large churches. 'I never saw anything more
beautiful than those burning buildings.'

By now the defenders of the bridge were being driven
from the houses as they caught fire. Their method of moving from one to another was, whenever possible, to
'mousehole'[8] their way from house to house in conditions
which grew steadily worse. During this tedious dusty
method of moving from one position to another Lieutenant
Simpson succeeded in disabling a tank close to the house in
which he was posted. Its crew got out and 'crept along the
wall till they came to a halt beneath the window where I was
crouching. I dropped a grenade on them and that was that. I
held it for two seconds before I let it drop'.

Two things were of particular concern: the lack of water,
and the breakdown of the wireless sets, which made it impossible to keep in touch with the rest of the division except
by means of the civilian telephone lines. These, manned by
the Dutch resistance, continued to play a part to the end,
the operators paying for their fortitude with their lives.
Frost had no continuous means of communicating with the
battalions which he still hoped were on their way to his
relief, but could sometimes speak with divisional headquarters. Perhaps the reinforcements were not very distant.
They might even be within earshot. 'During a lull we yelled
"Waho Mahommed",' says Briggs, 'hoping there would be
some reply. But none came. Then we tore down wallpaper
to make a megaphone six feet long, through which we
shouted words and epithets that could only be British.' But

there was still no reply.

Dawn on Wednesday, the 20th, shone on Frost, still clinging with difficulty to the north-west end of the bridge, but able to prevent the Germans crossing it. But now his personal good fortune was to desert him. During the morning he was badly wounded in the leg, and Major C. H. F. Gough, MC, Reconnaissance Squadron, assumed command, but still referred major decisions to Frost, while Tatham-Warter, 'whose conduct was exemplary even amid so much gallantry', took over what remained of the 2nd Battalion. In reporting these changes to the divisional commander at Hartestein, Gough referred to himself as 'the man who goes in for funny weapons', so that no German or collaborator listening in on the town exchange which he was using would be able to identify him.

The area occupied by the parachute troops grew smaller and smaller, though they continued to control the approaches to the bridge. Conspicuous among them at this stage was Lieutenant Grayburn of 'A' Company. Early in the action, in leading the unsuccessful attack on the south end of the bridge, he had been hit in the shoulder, but continued to lead his men and was the last to withdraw. He then established his platoon in a very exposed house whose position was vital to the defence. In this he held out until 19 September, when it was set on fire, having repelled all attacks, including those made by tanks and self-propelled guns. Reforming his depleted force, he was still able to maintain the defence and on 20 September led a series of fighting patrols, whose activities so galled the enemy that tanks were brought up again. Only then did Grayburn retreat and, even so, was still able to strike back. At the head of another patrol he drove off the enemy, thus allowing others to remove the fuses from the demolition charges which the Germans had succeeded in placing under the bridge. In so doing he was again wounded, but still would not leave the fight. Eventually, that evening he was killed by the fire of a tank. In his conduct 'he showed an example of devotion to duty which can seldom have been equalled', and was awarded a posthumous Victoria Cross.

By the evening of that day all the buildings near the bridge had been burnt down except the U-shaped school. This now caught fire and all attempts to put it out failed. Captain J. Logan, DSO, the medical officer, who with Captain D. Wright, MC, had been tireless in tending the wounded, therefore informed Gough that he must surrender them if he wished to save them from being burnt or roasted alive in the cellars. Just after dark, under a flag of truce, the enemy picked up many of the wounded, including Frost, who had been expecting his fate and had thrown away his badges. A moment before, Wicks, his batman, had taken leave of him and gone back to the fight. He, too, was soon afterwards badly wounded.

Gough and those still unwounded continued to resist. Though ammunition was practically at an end, they nevertheless succeeded in delivering an attack at dawn on 21 September in an attempt to retake some of the houses. It failed and what remained of the 2nd Battalion scattered in small parties in an endeavour to find their way to the XXX Corps, which they had awaited so long and so vainly. At last the bridge was once more in German hands.

In this action the 2nd Battalion had been wiped out; but seldom can a fighting unit of any army in any age have had so glorious an end. For thrice the length of time laid down in its orders it had held a bridge against odds which were overwhelming from the beginning. Buoyed up by hope and by frequent messages that relief or support was on the way, either at the hands of the rest of the 1st Parachute Brigade and later the 4th Brigade, or from XXX Corps moving up from Nijmegen, when that hope was deferred, the hearts of its officers and men were not sick. They continued to fight, and only ceased to fire when their ammunition was gone and their wounded, now the great majority, faced with a fearful and unnecessary death. The conduct of the 2nd Battalion at the Bridge at Arnhem is more than an inspiration or an example; it was the quintessence of all those qualities which the parachute soldier must possess and display if he is to justify his training and the trust reposed in him. So great a spirit in evidence every moment of those three September days and nights can be overcome only by weight of numbers. That, and that alone, was the cause of their glorious defeat.

The fighting was to continue for a further five days. From the outset of the operation the weather steadily deteriorated, interrupting support from the air and the dropping of supplies. Both sides continued to fight with tenacious courage, often with hand-to-hand clashes. Evacuation of the survivors of the 1st Airborne Division became inevitable, with one Panzer division steadily advancing into the area held in Arnhem and around the bridge and a second Panzer division barring the way for the XXX Corps still attempting to come to the rescue. On 25-26 September this Corps put up a heavy and prolonged barrage near Osterbeck, 6 kilometres down the Rhine west of Arnhem. Under this cover 2000 of the airborne troops who were still unwounded were evacuated. Operation Market Garden was over. Casualties in this, perhaps the fiercest battle of the war in the West, were enormous. The American Divisions lost 7000 men; 1200 of the British 1st Airborne were killed and 5200 injured or taken prisoner. German losses have never been accurately recorded, but were probably as great. The 9th Panzer Division, which fought around the bridge, alone lost 3500 men. Nearly seven months were to elapse before Arnhem was liberated. British and Canadian troops entered the town on 14 April 1945.

Notes

[1] Major B. A. Wilson, commanding 21st Independent Parachute Company.
[2] Battle during invasion of Sicily in 1943.
[3] Brigadier J. W. Hackett, commanding 4th Parachute Brigade.
[4] Lieutenant Colonel D. T. Dobie, 1st Airborne Battalion.
[5] Lieutenant Colonel W. D. McCardie.
[6] Lieutenant Colonel G. H. Lea.
[7] Lieutenant Colonel J. D. Frost, 2nd Parachute Battalion.
[8] Knocking or blowing a hole in the dividing walls and thus moving from house to house under cover.

More Beaver Books

We hope you have enjoyed this Beaver Book. Here are some of the other titles:

My Favourite Escape Stories   Pat Reid, author of *The Colditz Story*, presents his favourite true stories from 400 years of escapes. Gripping reading for everyone from nine upwards

The Beaver Book of Bikes   A Beaver original. Packed with information on everything you need to know about bicycles — from buying, maintenance and restoration to games, activities and the history of bikes — this book is written by Harry Hossent and illustrated with drawings by Peter Gregory and cartoons by Maggie Ling

It Figures!   A Beaver original. Did you know that you can make four 4s equal 64, add five odd numbers to make a total of 14, or multiply a three-digit number so the answer is the number repeated twice? This book is crammed with incredible calculations, tricks and games with numbers, to baffle and amaze your friends and keep you amused for hours. Written by Clive Dickinson and illustrated by Graham Thompson

These and many other Beavers are available from your local bookshop or newsagent, or can be ordered direct from: Hamlyn Paperback Cash Sales, PO Box 11, Falmouth, Cornwall TR10 9EN. Send a cheque or postal order, made payable to the Hamlyn Publishing Group, for the price of the book plus postage at the following rates:
UK: 40p for the first book, 18p for the second book, and 13p for each additional book ordered to a maximum charge of £1.49;
BFPO and Eire: 40p for the first book, 18p for the second book, plus 13p per copy for the next 7 books and thereafter 7p per book;
OVERSEAS: 60p for the first book and 18p for each extra book.

New Beavers are published every month and if you would like the *Beaver Bulletin*, a newsletter which tells you about new books and gives a complete list of titles and prices, send a large stamped addressed envelope to:

Beaver Bulletin
Hamlyn Paperbacks
Banda House
Cambridge Grove
London W6 0LE

20362X